The Story of a
Shipwrecked Sailor

GABRIEL
GARCÍA MÁRQUEZ

The Story of a
Shipwrecked Sailor

*who drifted on a life raft for ten days
without food or water, was proclaimed a national hero,
kissed by beauty queens, made rich through publicity,
and then spurned by the government
and forgotten for all time*

*Translated from the Spanish
by Randolph Hogan*

ALFRED A. KNOPF
NEW YORK 1986

THIS IS A BORZOI BOOK
PUBLISHED BY ALFRED A. KNOPF, INC.

Copyright ©1986 by Alfred A. Knopf, Inc.
Map copyright © 1986 by Rafael Palacios
All rights reserved under International and
Pan-American Copyright Conventions. Published
in the United States by Alfred A. Knopf, Inc.,
New York, and simultaneously in Canada by
Random House of Canada Limited, Toronto.
Distributed by Random House, Inc., New York.
Originally published in Spain as *Relato de un náufrago*
by Tusquets Editores, Barcelona.
Copyright © 1970 by Gabriel García Márquez.

Library of Congress Cataloging-in-Publication Data

García Márquez, Gabriel
The story of a shipwrecked sailor.

Translation of: Relato de un náufrago.
1. Velasco, Luis Alejandro.   2. Survival (after
airplane accidents, shipwrecks, etc.)   I. Title.
G530.V442G3713   1986   910'.091636   85-45673
ISBN 0-394-54810-8

Manufactured in the United States of America

The Story of This Story

February 28, 1955, brought news that eight crew members of the destroyer *Caldas*, of the Colombian Navy, had fallen overboard and disappeared during a storm in the Caribbean Sea. The ship was traveling from Mobile, Alabama, in the United States, where it had docked for repairs, to the Colombian port of Cartagena, where it arrived two hours after the tragedy. A search for the seamen began immediately, with the cooperation of the U.S. Panama Canal Authority, which performs such functions as military control and other humanitarian deeds in the southern Caribbean. After four days, the search was abandoned and the lost sailors were officially declared dead. A week later, however, one of them turned up half dead on a deserted beach in northern Colombia, having survived ten days without food or water on a drifting life raft. His name was Luis Alejandro Velasco. This book is a journalistic reconstruction of what he told me, as it was published one month after the disaster in the Bogotá daily *El Espectador*.

What neither the sailor nor I knew when we tried to reconstruct his adventure minute by minute was that our exhaustive digging would lead us to a new adventure that caused a certain stir in the nation and cost him his honor, and could have cost me my skin. At that time Colombia was under the military and social dictatorship of General Gustavo Rojas Pinilla, whose two most memorable feats were the killing of students in the center of the capital when the Army broke up a peaceful demonstration with bullets, and the assassination by the secret police of an undetermined number of Sunday bullfight fans who had booed the dictator's daughter at the bullring. The press was censored, and the daily problem for opposition newspapers was finding politically germ-free stories with which to entertain their readers. At *El Espectador*, those in charge of that estimable confectionary work were Guillermo Cano, director; José Salgar, editor-in-chief, and I, staff reporter. None of us was over thirty.

When Luis Alejandro Velasco showed up of his own accord to ask how much we would pay him for his story, we took it for what it was: a rehash. The armed forces had sequestered him for several weeks in a naval hospital, and he had been allowed to talk only with reporters favorable to the regime and with one opposition journalist who had disguised himself as a doctor. His story had been told piece-meal many times, had been pawed over and perverted, and readers seemed fed up with a hero who had rented himself out to advertise watches (because his watch hadn't even slowed down during the storm); who appeared in shoe advertisements (because his shoes were so sturdy that he hadn't been able to tear them apart to eat them); and who had performed many other publicity stunts. He had been decorated, he had made patriotic speeches on radio, he had been displayed on television as an example to future generations, and he had toured the country amid bouquets and fanfares, signing autographs and being kissed by beauty queens. He had amassed a small fortune. If he was now coming to us without our having invited him, after we had tried so hard to reach him earlier, it was likely that he no longer had much to tell, that he was capable of inventing anything for money, and that the government had very clearly defined the limits of what he could say. We sent him away. But on a hunch, Guillermo Cano caught up with him on the stairway, accepted the deal, and placed him in my hands. It was as if he had given me a time bomb.

My first surprise was that this solidly built twenty-year-old, who looked more like a trumpet player than a national hero, had an exceptional instinct for the art of narrative, an astonishing memory and ability to synthesize, and enough uncultivated dignity to be able to laugh at his own heroism. In twenty daily sessions, each lasting six hours, during which I took notes and sprang trick questions on him to expose contradictions, we put together an accurate and concise account of his ten days at sea. It was so detailed and so exciting that my only concern was finding readers who would believe it. Not solely for that reason but also because it seemed fitting, we agreed that the story would be written in the first person and signed by him. This is the first time my name has appeared in connection with the text.

The second, and more important, surprise occurred during the fourth day of work, when I asked Luis Alejandro Velasco to describe the storm that caused the disaster. Aware that his statement was worth its weight in gold, he answered with a smile, "There was no storm." It was true:

the weather bureau confirmed that it had been another clear and mild February in the Caribbean. The truth, never published until then, was that the ship, tossed violently by the wind in heavy seas, had spilled its ill-secured cargo and the eight sailors overboard. This revelation meant that three serious offenses had been committed: first, it was illegal to transport cargo on a destroyer; second, the overweight prevented the ship from maneuvering to rescue the sailors; and third, the cargo was contraband—refrigerators, television sets, and washing machines. Clearly, the account, like the destroyer, was loaded with an ill-secured moral and political cargo that we hadn't foreseen.

The story, divided into installments, ran for fourteen consecutive days. At first the government applauded the literary consecration of its hero. Later, when the truth began to emerge, it would have been politically dishonest to halt publication of the series: the paper's circulation had almost doubled, and readers scrambled in front of the building to buy back issues in order to collect the entire series. The dictatorship, in accordance with a tradition typical of Colombian governments, satisfied itself by patching up the truth with rhetoric: in a solemn statement, it denied that the destroyer had been loaded with contraband goods. Looking for a way to substantiate our charges, we asked Luis Alejandro Velasco for a list of his fellow crewmen who owned cameras. Although many of them were vacationing in various parts of the country, we managed to find them and buy the photographs they had taken during their voyage. One week after the publication of the series, the complete story appeared in a special supplement illustrated with the sailors' photographs. Behind the groups of friends on the high seas one could see the boxes of contraband merchandise and even, unmistakably, the factory labels. The dictatorship countered the blow with a series of drastic reprisals that would result, months later, in the shutdown of the newspaper. Despite the pressure, the threats, and the most seductive attempts at bribery, Luis Alejandro Velasco did not recant a word of his story. He had to leave the Navy, the only career he had, and disappeared into the oblivion of everyday life. After two years the dictatorship collapsed and Colombia fell to the mercy of other regimes that were better dressed but not much more just, while in Paris I began my nomadic and somewhat nostalgic exile that in certain ways also resembles a drifting raft. No one heard anything more about that lone sailor until a few months later, when a wandering journalist found him seated behind a desk at a bus company. I have seen the photograph taken of him then: he had grown older and heavier, and looked as if life had passed through him, leaving behind the serene aura of a hero who had had the courage to dynamite his own statue.

I have not reread this story in fifteen years. It seems worthy of publication, but I have never quite understood the usefulness of publishing it. I find it depressing that the publishers are not so much interested in the merit of the story as in the name of the author, which, much to my sorrow, is also that of a fashionable writer. If it is now published in the form of a book, that is because I agreed without thinking about it very much, and I am not a man to go back on his word.

G. G. M.

Barcelona, February 1970

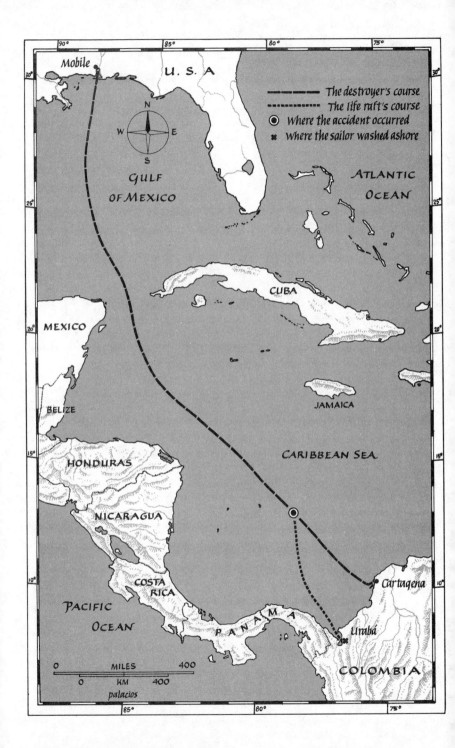

The Story of a
Shipwrecked Sailor

I

How My Shipmates Died at Sea

On February 22 we were told that we would be returning to Colombia. For eight months we had been in Mobile, Alabama, where the electronic equipment and gunnery of the *Caldas* were being repaired. While on liberty we did what all sailors do ashore: we went to the movies with our girlfriends and afterward met at a bar in the port, the Joe Palooka, where we drank whiskey and sometimes started brawls.

My girlfriend was named Mary Address, and I met her through another sailor's girlfriend after I had been in Mobile for two months. Mary had some fluency in Spanish, but I don't think she ever understood why my friends called her, in jest, "María Dirección." Each time we had shore leave I took her to the movies, although she preferred going out for ice cream. With my half-English and her half-Spanish we could just about make ourselves understood, but we always did understand each other, at the movies or eating ice cream.

There was only one time I didn't go out with Mary: the night we saw *The Caine Mutiny*. Some of my friends had heard it was a good movie about life aboard a minesweeper. That was the reason we went to see it. The best part of the movie, however, wasn't the minesweeper but the storm. We all agreed that the thing to do in a situation like that was to change the vessel's course, as the mutineers had done. But none of us had ever been in a storm like that one, so nothing in the movie impressed us as much as the storm did. When we returned to the ship that night, one of the sailors, Diego Velázquez, who was very impressed by the movie, figured that in just a few days we would be at sea and wondered, "What if something like that happened to us?"

I confess that the movie also made an impression on me. In the past eight months, I had grown unaccustomed to the sea. I wasn't afraid, for an instructor had shown us how to fend for ourselves in the event of a shipwreck. Nonetheless, the uneasiness I felt the night we saw *The Caine Mutiny* wasn't normal.

I don't mean to say that from that moment I began to anticipate the catastrophe, but I had never been so apprehensive before a voyage. When I was a child in Bogotá, looking at illustrations in books, it never occurred to me that one might encounter death at sea. On the contrary, I had a great deal of faith in the sea. And from the time I had enlisted in the Navy, two years before, I had never felt anxious during a voyage.

But I'm not ashamed to say that I felt something like fear after seeing *The Caine Mutiny*. Lying face up in my bunk, the uppermost one, I thought about my family and

about the voyage we would have to make before reaching
Cartagena. I couldn't sleep. With my head resting in my
hands, I listened to the soft splash of water against the
pier and the calm breathing of forty sailors sleeping in
their quarters. Just below my bunk, Seaman First Class
Luis Rengifo snored like a trombone. I don't know what
he was dreaming about, but he certainly wouldn't have
slept so soundly had he known that eight days later he
would be dead at the bottom of the sea.

My uneasiness lasted all through that week. The day of
departure was alarmingly close, and I tried to instill some
confidence in myself by talking to my mates. We talked
more insistently about our families, about Colombia, and
about our plans for our return. Little by little, the ship
was loaded with the gifts we would take home: radios,
refrigerators, washing machines, and stoves. I had bought
a radio.

Unable to shake off my worries, I made a resolution: as
soon as I reached Cartagena I would quit the Navy. The
night before we sailed I went to say goodbye to Mary. I
thought I would speak to her about my fears and about my
resolution. But I didn't, because I had promised her I'd
come back, and she wouldn't have believed me if I told her
I had decided never to sail again. The only person I did
tell was Seaman Second Class Ramón Herrera, who con-
fided that he, too, had decided to leave the Navy as soon
as we reached Cartagena. Sharing our misgivings, Ramón
Herrera and I went with Diego Velázquez to have a
whiskey and bid farewell to the Joe Palooka.

We thought we would have one whiskey, but we ended
up having five bottles. Practically all our girlfriends knew
we were leaving and they decided to say goodbye, get
drunk, and cry to show their gratitude. The bandleader, a

serious fellow who wore eyeglasses that made him look nothing like a musician, played a program of mambos and tangos in our honor, thinking this was Colombian music. Our girlfriends wept and drank whiskey at a dollar and a half a bottle.

Since we had been paid three times that week, we decided to raise the roof. Me, because I was worried and wanted to get drunk. Ramón Herrera, because he was happy, as always, and because he was from Arjona and knew how to play the drums and had a singular talent for imitating all the fashionable singers.

Shortly before we left, a North American sailor came up to our table and asked permission to dance with Ramón Herrera's girlfriend, an enormous blonde, the one who was drinking the least and crying the most—and she meant it! The North American asked permission in English and Ramón Herrera shook him, saying in Spanish, "I can't understand you, you son of a bitch!"

It turned out to be one of the best brawls Mobile ever had, with chairs broken over people's heads, radio patrol cars and cops. Ramón Herrera, who managed to throw a couple of good haymakers at the North American, went back to the ship at one in the morning, singing like Daniel Santos. He said it was the last time he would go aboard. And, indeed, it was.

At three in the morning on the twenty-fourth, the *Caldas* weighed anchor at Mobile, bound for Cartagena. We were all happy to be going home. And we were all taking along gifts. Chief Gunner's Mate Miguel Ortega seemed happiest of all. I don't think another sailor was ever as prudent as Miguel Ortega. During his eight months in Mobile he hadn't squandered a dollar. All the money he got he invested in presents for his wife, who was waiting for him in Cartagena. As we boarded that morning, Ortega was on the bridge, talking about his wife and children, which was no coincidence, because he never talked of anything else. He had a refrigerator, an automatic washer, a radio, and a stove for them. Twelve hours later, Ortega would be stretched out in his bunk, dying of seasickness. And twenty-four hours later, he would be dead at the bottom of the sea.

Death's guests

When a vessel weighs anchor, the order is issued: "Service personnel, to your stations." Everyone is supposed to remain at his station until the ship has left port. Standing quietly at my station in front of the torpedo tubes, I watched the lights of Mobile fade into the mist, but I wasn't thinking of Mary. I thought about the sea. I knew that on the following day we would be in the Gulf of Mexico, and at that time of year it was a dangerous route. Since dawn I hadn't seen Lieutenant Jaime Martínez Diago, second in command and the only officer to die in the catastrophe. He was tall and husky, a taciturn man whom I had seen on very few occasions. I knew that he was a native of Tolima and a fine person.

But that morning I did see First Warrant Officer Julio Amador Caraballo, a tall, well-built man, who passed by me, looking at the fading lights of Mobile, and went off to his station. I think it was the last time I saw him aboard the ship.

None of the crew of the *Caldas* was more vocal about his delight at going home than Warrant Officer Elías Sabogal, the chief engineer. He was a sea wolf. Small, leathery, robust, and talkative, he was about forty years old, and I think he had spent most of those years talking.

Sabogal had good reason to be happier than everyone else. In Cartagena his wife was waiting for him with their six children. He had seen only five of them, the youngest having been born while he was in Mobile.

The voyage was perfectly calm until dawn, and within an hour I had once again grown accustomed to sailing. To the east I could see the sun, just starting to rise. I wasn't feeling uneasy then, merely tired. I hadn't slept all night. I was thirsty and had bad memories of the whiskey of the night before.

At six the order was given: "Service personnel relieved. Midshipmen to your stations." As soon as I heard the order I returned to quarters. In the bunk below mine, Luis Rengifo, sitting up, blinked his eyes in an effort to wake up.

"Where are we going?" he asked.

I told him we had just left port. Then I climbed into my bunk and tried to go to sleep.

Luis Rengifo was a complete seaman. He was born in Chocó, which was far from the sea, but he had the sea in his blood. When the *Caldas* put in to Mobile for repairs, Luis Rengifo was not among the crew. He was in Washington, taking a course in armaments. He was serious, studious, and spoke English as well as he spoke Spanish.

He had received his civil engineering degree in Washington. He had also married a woman from the Dominican Republic there in 1952. When the repairs to the *Caldas* were completed, he left Washington and rejoined the crew. A few days before we left Mobile, he told me that the first thing he was going to do when he arrived in Colombia was to try to speed up the arrangements to have his wife move to Cartagena.

Since Luis Rengifo had not sailed for such a long time, I was sure he would be seasick. That first morning of the voyage he asked me, while he dressed, "Haven't you gotten sick yet?"

I told him I hadn't.

Then Rengifo said, "In two or three hours I'll see you with your tongue hanging out."

"That's how *you'll* look," I said.

"The day I'm sick," he replied, "the sea will get sick."

Lying in my bunk, trying to coax myself to sleep, I remembered the storm. My fears of the night before were rekindled. Worried again, I returned to where Luis Rengifo was dressing and said, "Be careful, now. Don't go letting your tongue punish you."

2

My Last Minutes Aboard the "Wolf Ship"

"We're in the Gulf now," one of my mates said when I awoke for breakfast on February 26. The day before, I had felt a little apprehensive about the weather in the Gulf of Mexico, but the destroyer, although it was rolling a little, slid along smoothly. I was happy that my fears had proved unfounded, and I went up on deck. The coastline had disappeared. Only the green sea and the blue sky stretched out ahead. Nevertheless, Miguel Ortega, pale and sickly-looking, was seated in the middle of the deck, struggling with seasickness. It had started sometime earlier, while the lights of Mobile were still visible, and for the last twenty-four hours Ortega had not been able to stand up, despite the fact that he wasn't a novice seaman.

Ortega had served in Korea, on the frigate *Almirante Padilla*. He had traveled a great deal and knew the sea well. But even though the Gulf was calm, he had to be helped from his station at the change of watch. He seemed to be in agony. He could not tolerate food, and his companions on watch had propped him up at the stern until they got an order to remove him to his bunk. Later he was stretched out there, face down, with his head hanging over the side, waiting to vomit.

I think it was Ramón Herrera who told me, on the night of the twenty-sixth, that things would get worse when we reached the Caribbean. According to our calculations, we would be leaving the Gulf of Mexico after midnight. At my watch station in front of the torpedo tubes, I thought optimistically about our arrival in Cartagena. The night was clear, and the high, round sky was filled with stars. From the time I joined the Navy, I had made a habit of identifying the stars, and that night I enjoyed doing it as the *Caldas* serenely made its way toward the Caribbean.

I think that an old sailor who has traveled the whole world can determine by the movement of his ship which sea he is sailing. My experience of the place where I had done my first sea duty told me we were in the Caribbean. I looked at my watch; it was half past midnight on the morning of February 27. I would have known we were in the Caribbean even if the ship wasn't rolling so much. But now I began to feel upset. I had a strange sense of premonition. And without knowing why, I thought of Chief Ortega, who was down below in his bunk, with his stomach in his mouth.

At six o'clock the destroyer began pitching violently. Luis Rengifo was awake, one bunk below me.

"Fatso," he asked me, "haven't you gotten sick yet?"

I said no, but I admitted I was worried. Rengifo, who, as I've said, was an engineer—very studious and a good seaman—explained why it was unlikely that something could happen to the *Caldas* in the Caribbean. "It's a wolf ship," he said. And then I remembered that during the war the destroyer had sunk a German submarine in these same waters.

"It's a safe ship," Luis Rengifo said. And, lying in my bunk, unable to sleep because of the rocking of the ship, I felt reassured by his words. But the wind grew stronger on the port side, and I imagined what might happen to the *Caldas* in those tremendous breakers. At that moment I remembered *The Caine Mutiny*.

But the weather hadn't changed all day, and our voyage was normal. When I relieved the watch, I kept busy thinking about what I would do when we reached Cartagena. First, I would write to Mary. I thought I would write to her twice a week, because I wasn't lazy about letters. Ever since I joined the Navy I had written to my family in Bogotá every week and regularly sent letters to friends in my neighborhood, Olaya. I would write Mary when we got to Cartagena—I figured out exactly how many hours it would take us to get there: twenty-four. That was the last thing I did on this watch.

Ramón Herrera helped me carry Miguel Ortega back to his bunk. He was worse. He had had no food since leaving Mobile three days before. He could barely speak, and he looked green and decidedly under the weather.

The dance begins

The dance began at 10 p.m. The *Caldas* had been swaying all day, but not as badly as on that night of the twenty-seventh. As I lay awake in my bunk, fearing for the crewmen on watch, I realized that none of the sailors lying in their bunks had been able to get to sleep. A little before midnight, I asked Luis Rengifo in the bunk below me, "Haven't you gotten sick yet?"

As I suspected, he hadn't been able to sleep either. But despite the lurching of the ship, he hadn't lost his sense of humor. He said, "I told you, the day I'm sick, the sea itself will be sick." It was a phrase he repeated often. But that night he barely had a chance to finish what he was saying.

I have said I was uneasy. I have said that I felt something akin to fear. But I have no doubts about what I felt after midnight on the twenty-seventh, when over the loudspeakers came the general order: "All personnel to the port side."

I understood what that order meant. The boat was listing dangerously to starboard and we were trying to right her with our weight. For the first time in two years of sailing, I was truly afraid of the sea. The wind whistled up on deck, where the crew would be soaked and shivering.

The moment I heard the order, I jumped out of my bunk. Very calmly, Luis Rengifo got up and went to one of the portside bunks, which was vacant because it belonged to one of the men on watch. Holding on to the other bunks, I tried to walk, but at that moment I remembered Miguel Ortega.

He couldn't move. When he heard the order, he tried to get up but fell back into his bunk, overcome by seasickness and exhaustion. I helped him sit up and secured him in the portside bunk. In a very low voice he told me he was ill.

"Let's arrange it so you don't have to go on watch," I said.

It seems like a bad joke, but if Miguel Ortega had stayed in his bunk he would still be alive.

Without even a minute's sleep, six of us who were on call assembled on the stern deck at 4 a.m. on the twenty-eighth. One was Ramón Herrera, my companion the whole time. The watch officer was Guillermo Rozo. It was my last duty on board. I knew that at two in the afternoon we would arrive at Cartagena. I thought that I would go to sleep as soon as I was relieved on watch, so that I could go out and enjoy myself on my home ground after an eight-month absence. At five-thirty I went on an inspection tour belowdecks, accompanied by a cabin boy. At seven we relieved those on active duty so that they could go to breakfast. At eight, they came back to relieve us. That was my last watch. Nothing unusual had happened, even though the wind was gaining force and the waves were getting bigger and bigger, crashing on the bridge and washing over the deck.

Ramón Herrera was at the stern. Luis Rengifo was there, too, as a lifeguard, with headphones in place. Lying down in the center of the deck, still in agony with his seasickness, was Miguel Ortega. That was the spot where the ship felt most stable. I talked a little with Seaman Second Class Eduardo Castillo from supply, a very reserved man and a bachelor from Bogotá. I don't remember what we talked about. All I know is that we didn't see each other again until he plunged into the sea a few hours later.

Ramón Herrera was collecting some cartons to cover himself with while he tried to get some sleep. With the rolling of the ship it was impossible to sleep in our quarters. The waves, getting taller and more powerful, swept over the deck. Amid the refrigerators, washing machines, and stoves that were tightly secured on the stern deck, Ramón Herrera and I lay down, carefully positioning ourselves to avoid being swept away by a wave. I looked up at the sky.

In this position I felt more secure, certain that in a few hours we would be reaching the bay of Cartagena. There was no storm; the day was perfectly clear, visibility total, and the sky a deep blue. Now, my boots weren't even hurting me, for I had changed into a pair of rubber-soled shoes after going off watch.

A moment of silence

Luis Rengifo asked me the time. It was eleven-thirty. An hour had passed since the ship had begun to list, leaning dangerously to starboard. The order of the previous night was repeated over the loudspeakers: "All personnel to the port side." Ramón Herrera and I didn't move, because we were already on that side.

I thought about Miguel Ortega, whom I had seen on the starboard side. But almost at the same moment, I saw him go reeling past me. He bent over the port side, in agony with his seasickness. At that moment the ship tilted frightfully; he was gone. I stopped breathing. A huge wave crashed over us and we were drenched, as though we had just come out of the sea. Very slowly, the ship labored to right itself. Luis Rengifo was ashen. Nervously he said, "What luck. This ship is going down and doesn't want to come back up."

That was the first time I had seen Luis Rengifo look nervous. Beside me, Ramón Herrera, deep in thought, completely soaked, remained quiet. There was a moment of total silence. Then Ramón Herrera said, "When they give the order to cut the ropes to release the cargo, I'll be the first one cutting them."

It was 11:50. I, too, thought that they would order the

ropes cut at any moment. That's what's called "lightening the decks." Radios, refrigerators, and stoves would slide into the sea as soon as the order was given. When that happened, I thought, I would have to go below to quarters, because we had been using the refrigerators and stoves to make ourselves secure on deck. Without them, the waves would have swept us away.

The ship continued to fight the waves, but it was listing more all the time. Ramón Herrera rolled up a tarpaulin and covered himself with it. Another wave, bigger than the previous one, crashed over us, but now we were protected by the canvas. I put my arms over my head while the wave passed, and half a minute later the loudspeakers barked.

They're going to give the order to cut the cargo loose, I thought. But it was a different order, spoken in a calm, confident voice: "Personnel on deck, don your life jackets."

Calmly, Luis Rengifo held his headphones in one hand and put on his life jacket with the other. First I felt a great emptiness, and then a profound silence, as I had after each enormous wave. I looked at Luis Rengifo, who, his life jacket on, had replaced his headphones. Then I closed my eyes. I could clearly hear the ticking of my watch.

I listened to the ticking for approximately one more minute. Ramón Herrera didn't move. I calculated that it must be almost twelve. Two hours to Cartagena. For a second, the ship seemed suspended in air. I started to raise my arm to look at my watch, but at that moment I couldn't see my arm, or my watch, either. I didn't see the wave. I felt the ship give way completely and the cargo that was supporting me slide away. I stood up, and in a fraction of a second the water was up to my neck. Then I saw Luis Rengifo, eyes popping, green and silent, trying to stay afloat, holding his headphones aloft. Then the water covered me completely and I started to swim toward the surface.

I swam upward for one, two, three seconds. I tried to reach the surface. I needed air. I was suffocating. I tried to grab hold of the cargo, but the cargo wasn't there anymore. Now there was nothing around me. When I got to the surface, I couldn't make out anything in the sea. A second later, about a hundred meters way, the ship surged up between the waves, gushing water from all sides like a submarine. It was only then that I realized I had fallen overboard.

3

Watching Four of My Shipmates Drown

My first impression was that I was utterly alone in the middle of the ocean. Trying to stay afloat, I watched another wave crash against the destroyer. The ship, now about two hundred meters from me, plunged into an abyss and disappeared from sight. I thought it had gone under. And a moment later, as if to confirm what I had thought, all the crates of merchandise that had been loaded onto the destroyer in Mobile began to surface and floated toward me, one by one. I kept afloat by grabbing on to the crates of clothing, radios, refrigerators, and other household goods that bounced around, willy-nilly, battered by the waves. I had no idea what was happening; a bit stunned, I took hold of one of the bobbing crates and stupidly began to contemplate the sea. It was a perfectly clear day. Except for the choppy waves produced by the wind and the cargo scattered across the surface, there was no evidence of a shipwreck.

Soon I began to hear shouts nearby. Through the sharp whistling of the wind, I recognized the voice of Julio Amador Caraballo, the tall, well-built first warrant officer, who was yelling at someone: "Grab hold there, under the life preserver."

It was as if in that instant I had awakened from a moment's deep sleep. It dawned on me that I wasn't alone in the sea. There, only a few meters away, my mates were shouting to one another and trying to stay afloat. Quickly, I began to think. I couldn't swim in just any direction. I knew we were about fifty miles from Cartagena, but I was not yet frightened. For a moment I thought I could hold on to the crate indefinitely, until help arrived. It was reassuring to know that all around me other sailors were in the same predicament. That was when I saw the raft.

There were two life rafts about seven meters apart. They appeared unexpectedly on the crest of a wave, near where my mates were calling out. It seemed odd that none of them could reach the life rafts. In an instant, one of the rafts disappeared from view. I couldn't decide whether to risk swimming toward the other one or stay safely anchored to my crate. But before I had time to decide, I found myself swimming toward the one I could see, which was moving farther away from me. I swam for about three minutes. I lost sight of the raft momentarily, but I was careful not to lose my bearings. Suddenly, a rough wave pushed the raft alongside me—it was huge, white, and empty. I struggled to grab the rigging and jump aboard. I made it on the third try. Once on the raft, panting, whipped by the wind, immobilized and freezing, I found it hard to sit up. Then I saw three of my mates near the raft, trying to reach it.

I recognized them immediately. Eduardo Castillo, the

quartermaster, had a firm grip around Julio Amador Caraballo's neck. Caraballo, who had been on watch when the accident occurred, was wearing his life jacket. He yelled: "Hold on tight, Castillo." They floated amid the scattered cargo, about ten meters away.

On the other side was Luis Rengifo. Only a few minutes before, I had seen him on the destroyer, trying to stay above water with his headphones aloft in his right hand. With his habitual calm, with that good sailor's confidence that allowed him to boast that the sea would get seasick before he did, he had stripped off his shirt so that he could swim better, but he had lost his life jacket. Even if I hadn't seen him, I would have recognized his cry: "Fatso, paddle over here."

I quickly grabbed the oars and tried to get closer to the men. Julio Amador, with Eduardo Castillo clinging to his neck, neared the raft. Much farther away, looking small and desolate, was the fourth of my mates: Ramón Herrera, who was waving at me while he held on to a crate.

Only three meters!

If I had had to decide, I wouldn't have known which of my mates to go after first. But when I saw Ramón Herrera, of the revel in Mobile, the happy young man from Arjona who had been with me on the stern only a few moments before, I began to paddle furiously. But the life raft was almost two meters long. It was very heavy in that lurching sea, and I had to row against the wind. I don't think I managed to advance more than a meter. Desperate, I looked around once more and saw that Ramón Herrera had disappeared. Only Luis Rengifo was swimming confidently toward the raft. I was sure he would make it. I had heard him snoring below my bunk, and I was convinced that his serenity was stronger than the sea.

In contrast, Julio Amador was struggling with Eduardo Castillo, so that Castillo wouldn't let go of his neck. They were less than three meters away. I figured that if they got just a little closer, I could hold out an oar for them to grab. But at that moment a gigantic wave lifted the raft, and from the top of the huge crest I could see the mast of the destroyer, heading away from me. When I came down again, Julio Amador had vanished, with Eduardo Castillo hanging on to his neck. Alone, two meters away, Luis Rengifo was still swimming calmly toward the raft.

I don't know why I did this absurd thing: knowing I couldn't move forward, I put the oar in the water as though trying to prevent the raft from moving, trying to anchor it in place. Luis Rengifo, exhausted, paused a moment, then raised his arm as he had when he held his headphones aloft, and shouted again: "Row over here, Fatso!"

The wind was blowing from his direction. I yelled that I couldn't row against the wind, that he should make another try, but I felt he hadn't heard me. The crates of cargo had disappeared and the life raft danced from side to side, battered by the waves. In an instant I was five meters away from Luis Rengifo and had lost sight of him. But he appeared in another spot, still not panicking, ducking underwater to prevent the waves from sweeping him away. I stood up, holding out the oar, hoping Luis Rengifo could get close enough to reach it. But then I could see he was tiring, losing heart. He called to me again, sinking: "Fatso! Fatso!"

I tried to row, but . . . it was as hopeless as the first time. I made a last try so that Luis Rengifo could reach the oar, but the raised hand, which a few minutes earlier had been trying to keep the headphones from sinking, sank forever, less than two meters from the oar.

I don't know how long I stayed like that, balancing in the life raft, holding out the oar. I kept searching the water, hoping that someone would surface soon. But the sea was clear and the wind, getting stronger, blew against my shirt like the howl of a dog. The cargo had disappeared. The mast, growing more distinct, proved that the destroyer hadn't sunk, as I had first thought. I felt calm. I thought that in a minute they would come looking for me. I thought that one of my mates had managed to reach the other life raft.

There was no reason they shouldn't have reached it. The rafts weren't provisioned—in fact, none of the destroyer's life rafts was outfitted. But there were six of them, apart from the rowboats and the whalers. It was reasonable to believe that some of my mates had reached the other life rafts, as I had reached mine, and perhaps the destroyer was searching for us.

Very soon I was aware of the sun. A midday sun, hot and metallic. Stupefied, not fully recovered, I looked at my watch. It was noon on the dot.

Alone

The last time Luis Rengifo had asked me the time, on the destroyer, it was 11:30. I had checked the time again, at 11:50, and the disaster had not yet occurred. When I looked at my watch on the life raft, it was exactly noon. It had taken only ten minutes for everything to happen—for me to reach the life raft, and try to rescue my shipmates, and stand motionless in the raft, searching the empty sea, listening to the sharp howl of the wind. I thought it would take them at least two or three hours to rescue me.

Two or three hours, I calculated. It seemed an extraordinarily long time to be alone at sea. But I tried to resign myself to it. I had no food or water, and by three in the afternoon I would surely have a searing thirst. The sun burned my head and my skin, which was dry and hardened by salt. Since I had lost my cap, I splashed water on my head, and I just sat on the side of the raft, waiting to be rescued.

It was only then that I felt the pain in my right knee. The thick, blue drill fabric of my trouser leg was wet, so I had a hard time rolling it up. But when I did, I was startled: I saw a deep, half-moon-shaped wound on the lower part of my knee. I didn't know if I had gashed it on the side of the ship, or if it had happened when I hit the water, for I didn't notice it until I was seated in the life raft. Though the wound burned a little, it had stopped bleeding and was completely dry, because of the salt water, I imagine.

Uncertain as to what to do, I decided to make an inventory of my belongings. I wanted to figure out what I could count on in my solitude at sea. First of all, I could rely on my watch, which kept perfect time, and which I couldn't stop glancing at every two or three minutes. In addition, I had my gold ring, which I'd bought in Cartagena the year before, and a chain with a medal of the Virgin of Carmen on it, also purchased in Cartagena, from another sailor for thirty-five pesos. In my pockets I had nothing but the keys to my locker on the destroyer and three business cards I had been given at a store in Mobile one day in January when I had gone out shopping with Mary Address. Since I had nothing to do, I read the cards over and over to distract myself until I was rescued. I don't know why the cards seemed like the messages in bottles that shipwrecked sailors pitch into the sea. I think if I had had a bottle at that moment I would have put one of the cards into it, playing shipwrecked sailor, just to do something amusing to tell my friends about in Cartagena.

4

My First Night Alone in the Caribbean

The wind died down by four in the afternoon. Since I could see nothing but water and sky, since I had no points of reference, more than two hours had passed before I realized that the raft was moving. But, in fact, from the moment I had found myself in it, the raft had been moving ahead in a straight line, pushed by the breeze faster than I could have pushed it with the oars. Nevertheless, I hadn't the faintest idea of my direction or position. I didn't know if the raft was moving in toward the shore or out toward the middle of the Caribbean. The latter seemed more likely, because I had always thought it was impossible for the sea to wash ashore anything that was fifty miles out, and even less likely if the object was as heavy as a man in a life raft.

During the next two hours I plotted the destroyer's voyage in my mind, minute by minute. I reasoned that if the radio operator had contacted Cartagena, he would have relayed the exact position of the accident and at that moment planes and helicopters would have been sent out to rescue us. I calculated that the planes would be there within an hour, circling over my head.

At one in the afternoon I sat down in the raft to scan the horizon. I stowed the three oars inside, ready to row toward wherever the planes appeared. The minutes were long and intense. The sun seared my face and shoulders, and my lips burned, split by the salt. But I felt neither thirst nor hunger. My only need was for the planes to turn up. I already had a plan: when I saw them I would try to row toward them; then, when they were overhead, I would stand up in the raft and signal to them with my shirt. To be prepared and not waste even a moment, I unbuttoned my shirt. Then I just sat on the edge of the raft, searching the horizon on all sides, because I hadn't the slightest idea from which direction the planes would appear.

It was two o'clock. The wind went on roaring, and above the noise I could still hear the voice of Luis Rengifo: "Fatso! Row over this way." I heard it with perfect clarity, as if he were there, only two meters away, trying to reach the oar. But I know that when the wind howls at sea, that when the waves break against the cliffs, one hears voices from memory. And you go on hearing them, with maddening persistence: "Row over here, Fatso!"

At three I began to get desperate. I knew that by then the destroyer would be docked at Cartagena. My mates, happy to be back, would be spreading out all over the city. I felt they were all thinking about me, and the thought gave me the energy and patience to hold on until four. Even if they hadn't radioed, even if they hadn't noticed that we'd gone overboard, they would have realized it the moment they docked, when the entire crew should have been on deck. That would have been at three o'clock, at the latest; they would have given the alert immediately.

However long the planes might have been delayed taking off, they should have been flying near the site of the accident within half an hour. So at four o'clock—four-fifteen at the latest—they would be circling over my head. I went on searching the horizon, until the breeze stopped and I felt enveloped in a great silence.

Only then did I stop hearing Luis Rengifo's cry.

The great night

At first it seemed impossible that I had been alone at sea for three hours. But at five o'clock, after five hours had passed, it seemed I might have to wait yet another hour. The sun was setting. It got very big and red in the west, and I began to orient myself. Now I knew where the planes would appear: with the sun to my left, I stared straight ahead, not moving, not daring to blink, not diverting my sight for an instant from the direction in which, by my bearings, Cartagena lay. By six o'clock my eyes hurt. But I kept watching. Even after it began to get dark, I watched with stubborn patience. I knew I wouldn't be able to see the planes, but I would spot their red and green lights heading toward me before I heard the noise of the engines. I wanted to see the lights, forgetting that, in the darkness, no one in the planes would see me. Soon the sky turned red, and I continued to search the horizon. Then it turned a deep violet as I kept watching. To one side of the life

raft, like a yellow diamond in a wine-colored sky, the first
star appeared, immobile and perfect. It was like a signal:
immediately afterward, night fell.

The first thing I felt, plunged into darkness so thick I
could no longer see the palm of my hand, was that I
wouldn't be able to overcome the terror. From the slapping
of the waves against the sides, I knew the raft was moving,
slowly but inexorably. Sunk in darkness, I realized I hadn't
felt so alone in the daytime. I was more alone in the dark,
in a raft that I could no longer see but could feel beneath
me, gliding silently over a dense sea filled with strange
creatures. To make myself less lonely, I looked at the dial
of my watch. It was ten minutes to seven. Much later—it
seemed as if two or three hours had passed—it was five
minutes to seven. When the minute hand reached twelve,
it was exactly seven o'clock and the sky was packed with
stars. But to me it seemed that so much time had passed,
it should now be nearly dawn. Desperately I went on
thinking about the planes.

I started to feel cold. In a life raft it's impossible to stay
dry even for a minute. Even if you are seated on the gunwale, half your body is underwater because the bottom of
the raft is shaped like a basket, extending more than half
a meter below the surface. By eight o'clock the water was
not as cold as the air. I knew that at the bottom of the
raft I was safe from sea creatures because the rope mesh
that protected the bottom prevented them from coming
too close. But that's what you learn in school, and that's
what you believe in school, when the instructor puts on
a demonstration with a scale model of the life raft and
you're seated on a bench among forty classmates at two
o'clock in the afternoon. When you're alone at sea at eight

o'clock at night, and without hope, the instructor's words make no sense at all. I knew that half of my body was in a realm that didn't belong to men but to the creatures of the sea, and that despite the icy wind whipping my shirt, I didn't dare move from the gunwale. According to the instructor, that was the least safe part of the raft. But all things considered, it was only there that I felt far enough away from the creatures: those immense unknown beasts I could hear passing the raft.

That night I had trouble finding Ursa Minor, lost in an endless maze of stars. I had never seen so many. It was hard to locate an empty space in the entire span of the sky. Once I spotted Ursa Minor, I didn't dare look anywhere else. I don't know why I felt less alone looking at Ursa Minor.

On shore leave in Cartagena, we often gathered at the Manga bridge in the small hours to listen to Ramón Herrera sing, imitating Daniel Santos while someone accompanied him on the guitar. Sitting on the wall of the stone bridge, I always found Ursa Minor on one side of the Cerro de la Popa. That night, sitting on the gunwale of the raft, I felt for a moment as if I were back at the Manga bridge, with Ramón Herrera next to me singing to a guitar, and as if Ursa Minor weren't two hundred miles from Earth but, instead, up on top of the Cerro de la Popa itself. I imagined someone in Cartagena looking at Ursa Minor while I watched it from the sea, and that made me feel less lonely.

My first night at sea seemed very long because absolutely nothing happened. It is impossible to describe a night on a life raft, when nothing happens and you're scared of unseen creatures and you've got a watch with a glowing dial that you can't stop checking even for a minute. The night of February 28—my first night at sea—I looked at my watch every minute. It was torture. In desperation, I swore I would stop doing it and I'd stow the watch in my pocket, so as not to be so dependent on the time. I was able to resist until twenty to nine. I still wasn't hungry or thirsty, and I was sure I could hold out until the following day, when the planes would arrive. But I thought the watch would drive me crazy. A prisoner of anxiety, I took it off my wrist to stuff it in my pocket, but as I held it in my hand it occurred to me that it would be better to fling it into the sea. I hesitated a moment. Then I was terrified: I thought I would feel even more alone without the watch. I put it back on my wrist and began to look at it again, minute by minute, as I had in the afternoon when I searched the horizon for airplanes until my eyes began to hurt.

After midnight I wanted to cry. I hadn't slept for a moment, but I hadn't even wanted to. With the same hope I had felt in the afternoon as I waited for airplanes, that night I looked for the lights of ships. For hours I scrutinized the sea, a tranquil sea, immense and silent, but I didn't see a single light other than the stars.

The cold was more intense in the early hours of morning, and it seemed as if my body were glowing, with all the sun of the afternoon embedded under my skin. With the cold, it burned more intensely. From midnight on, my right knee began to hurt and I felt as though the water had penetrated to my bones. But these feelings were remote: I thought about my body less than about the lights of the ships. It seemed to me, in the midst of that infinite solitude, in the midst of the sea's dark murmur, that if I spotted the light of only a single ship, I would let out a yell that could be heard at any distance.

The light of each day

Dawn did not break slowly, as it does on land. The sky turned pale, the first stars disappeared, and I went on looking, first at my watch and then at the horizon. The contours of the sea began to appear. Twelve hours had passed, but it didn't seem possible. Night couldn't be as long as day. You have to have spent the night at sea, sitting in a life raft and looking at your watch, to know that the night is immeasurably longer than the day. But soon dawn begins to break, and then it's wearying to know it's another day.

That occurred to me on my first night in the raft. When dawn came, nothing else mattered. I thought neither of water nor of food. I didn't think of anything at all, until the wind turned warmer and the sea's surface grew smooth and golden. I hadn't slept a second all night, but at that moment it seemed as if I'd just awakened. When I stretched out in the raft my bones ached and my skin burned. But the day was brilliant and warm, and the murmur of the wind picking up gave me a new strength to continue waiting. And I felt profoundly composed in the life raft. For the first time in my twenty years of life, I was perfectly happy.

The raft continued to drift forward—how far it had gone during the night I couldn't calculate—but the horizon still looked exactly the same, as if I hadn't moved a centimeter. At seven o'clock I thought of the destroyer. It was breakfast time. I imagined my shipmates seated around the table eating apples. Then we would have eggs. Then meat. Then bread and coffee. My mouth filled with saliva and I could feel a slight twisting in my stomach. To take my mind off the idea of food, I submerged myself up to my neck in the bottom of the raft. The cool water on my sunburned back was soothing and made me feel stronger. I stayed submerged like that for a long time, asking myself why I had gone with Ramón Herrera to the stern deck instead of returning to my bunk to lie down. I reconstructed the tragedy minute by minute and decided I had been stupid. There was really no reason I should have been one of the victims: I wasn't on watch, I wasn't required on deck. When I concluded that everything that had happened was due to bad luck, I felt anxious again. But looking at my watch calmed me down. The day was moving along quickly: it was eleven-thirty.

A black speck on the horizon

The approach of midday made me think about Cartagena again. I thought it was impossible they hadn't noticed I was missing. I began regretting that I had made it to the life raft; I imagined that my shipmates had been rescued and that I was the only one still adrift because my raft had been blown away by the wind. I even attributed reaching the life raft to bad luck.

That idea had hardly ripened when I thought I saw a speck on the horizon. I fixed my sights on the black point coming toward me. It was eleven-fifty. I watched so intently that the sky was soon filled with glittering points. But the black speck kept moving closer, heading directly toward the raft. Two minutes after I spotted it, I could make out its form perfectly. As it approached from the sky, luminous and blue, it threw off blinding, metallic flashes. Little by little I could distinguish it from the other bright specks. My neck started to hurt and my eyes could no longer tolerate the sky's brilliance. But I kept on looking: it was fast and gleaming, and it was coming directly toward the raft. At that moment I wasn't feeling happy. I felt no overwhelming emotion. I had a sense of great clarity and I felt extraordinarily calm as I stood in the raft while the plane approached. I took off my shirt slowly. I felt that I knew the exact moment when I should begin signaling with it. I stood there a minute, two minutes, with the shirt in my hand, waiting for the plane to come closer. It headed directly toward the raft. When I raised my arm and began to wave the shirt, I could hear, over the noise of the waves, the vibration of the plane's engines grow louder.

5

A Companion Aboard the Life Raft

For at least five minutes I waved my shirt furiously, but I quickly saw I had been mistaken: the plane wasn't coming toward the raft at all. As I watched the black speck growing larger, it seemed as if the plane would fly overhead. But it passed far away, too high to see me. Then it made a wide turn, started to head back, and disappeared into the sky from where it had appeared. Standing in the raft, exposed to the scorching sun, I looked at the black speck, not thinking about anything, as it erased itself completely from the horizon. Then I sat down again. I was disheartened, and though I hadn't given up hope, I decided to take precautions to protect myself from the sun. In the first place, I shouldn't let my lungs be exposed to the sun's rays.

I had spent exactly twenty-four hours aboard the raft. I lay supine on its side and put the damp shirt over my face. I didn't try to sleep, because I knew the danger that awaited me if I dozed off on the raft's gunwale. I thought about the plane: I wasn't sure they were searching for me, and I couldn't identify the plane.

There, lying on the gunwale, I began to feel the torture of thirst. At first it was thick saliva and dryness in my throat. It made me want to drink sea water, but I knew that would be harmful. I could drink some later on. Soon I forgot about thirst. Directly overhead, louder than the sound of the waves, I heard another plane.

Excited, I sat up. The plane approached, from the same direction as the other plane, but this one was flying right toward the raft. The moment it passed overhead I waved my shirt again. But the plane was flying very high. It was far away; it flew off, disappeared. Then it returned, and I saw it in profile against the sky, flying back in the direction from which it had come: Now they're looking for me, I thought. And I waited on the gunwale, shirt in hand, for more planes to come.

One thing about the aircraft became clear: they appeared and disappeared at a single point. So land was in that direction. Now I knew what course to follow. But how? Even though the raft had traveled a lot during the night, it must still be a long way from the coast. Now I knew in which direction it lay, but I had no idea how far I would have to row, with the sun beginning to give me chicken skin and my stomach aching from hunger. Above all, there was the thirst. And it was becoming harder to breathe all the time.

About 12:35—I didn't notice the exact time—a huge black plane, with pontoons for landing in the water, roared directly overhead. My heart leaped. I saw it distinctly. The day was so clear I could see a man looking out of the cockpit, searching the ocean with a pair of black binoculars. The plane flew so low, so close to me, I thought

I could feel a gust of wind on my face from one of its engines. I identified it clearly by the letters on its wings: it was a plane from the Canal Zone Coast Guard.

As it turned back buzzing toward the interior of the Caribbean, I didn't for a moment doubt that the man with the binoculars had seen me waving my shirt. "They've found me!" I shouted, still waving the shirt. Crazed with excitement, I jumped up and down in the raft.

They've spotted me!

In less than five minutes the black plane came back and flew in the opposite direction, at the same altitude as before. It banked to the left, and in the window on that side I again clearly saw the man searching the sea with his binoculars. I waved my shirt again. But now I wasn't shaking it desperately. I waved it calmly, not as if I were asking for help, but as if I were enthusiastically greeting and thanking my rescuers.

Although the plane was coming closer, it looked as if it were losing altitude. For a moment it flew in a straight line, almost on the surface of the water. I thought it was going to land, and I got ready to row toward the place where it would touch down. But a moment later it began climbing, then turned around and flew overhead a third time, so I didn't wave my shirt vigorously. When the plane was directly over the raft I gave a brief signal and waited for it to pass again, lower down. But just the opposite happened: it climbed rapidly and headed back toward the place from which it had appeared. Still, I had no reason to worry. I was sure they had seen me. It was impossible that they hadn't, flying so low and directly over the raft. Reassured, unworried, and happy, I sat down to wait.

An hour passed. I reached a very important conclusion: the point from which the planes had first appeared was undoubtedly Cartagena. The point where the black plane had disappeared was over Panama. I calculated that, rowing in a straight line, and detouring a little from the force of the wind, I would probably reach the resort of Tolú. That was more or less midway between the two points.

I thought I would be rescued within an hour. But the hour passed without anything occurring in the blue sea, which was clear and perfectly calm. Two more hours went by. And another, and another. I didn't move from the gunwale for a second. I was tense, scrutinizing the horizon without even blinking. The sun began to set at five o'clock. Although I hadn't given up hope, I was beginning to feel uneasy. I was sure they had seen me from the black plane, but I couldn't understand why so much time had gone by without their coming to rescue me. My throat was completely dry. It was even getting harder to breathe. I was distractedly looking at the horizon when, without knowing why, I jumped up and fell into the middle of the raft. Slowly, as if hunting its quarry, a shark slid by the side of the raft.

The sharks arrive at five

It was the first creature I had seen after thirty hours on the raft. A shark fin inspires terror because one knows how voracious the beast is. But in fact, nothing appears more innocuous than a shark fin. It doesn't look like part of an animal, even less part of a savage beast. It's green and rough, like the bark of a tree. As I watched it edge past the side of the raft, I imagined it might have a fresh flavor, somewhat bitter, like the skin of a vegetable. It was after five. The sea was tranquil in the afternoon light. More sharks approached the raft, patiently marauding until darkness fell. Then there was no more light, but I sensed them circling in the darkness, tearing the calm surface with the blades of their fins.

From that point on, I stopped sitting on the edge of the raft after five in the afternoon. Over the next few days I would learn that sharks are punctual creatures: they would arrive a little after five and vanish by nightfall.

At twilight the transparent sea provided a lovely spectacle. Fish of every color approached the raft. Enormous yellow and green fish, fish striped in blue and red, round ones and little ones, accompanied the raft until dark. Sometimes there was a metallic flash, a spurt of bloody water would gush on board, and pieces of a fish destroyed by a shark would float by. Then countless smaller fish would appear among the remains. At such times I would have sold my soul for the smallest piece of the shark's leftovers.

My second night at sea was one of hunger and thirst and desperation. I felt abandoned, clinging only to my hope that I would be rescued. That night I decided that all I could rely on to save myself were my will and what was left of my strength.

One thing astounded me: I felt a little weak, but not exhausted. I had endured nearly forty hours without water or food and more than two days and two nights without sleep, and I had been awake the entire night before the accident. Nonetheless, I felt capable of rowing.

Again I searched for Ursa Minor. I fixed my sights on it

and began to row. There was a breeze, but it wasn't blowing in the direction I should have been going in to navigate directly toward Ursa Minor. I secured both oars to the gunwale and decided to row until ten o'clock. At first I rowed furiously, then more calmly, my eyes fixed on Ursa Minor, which according to my calculations shone directly over the Cerro de la Popa.

From the sound of the water, I knew I was moving forward. When I got tired I crossed the oars and laid my head down to rest. Then I grabbed the oars more firmly and more hopefully. At midnight I was still rowing.

A companion

Around two o'clock I was completely exhausted. I crossed the oars and tried to sleep. My thirst was great, but hunger didn't bother me. I was so tired that I rested my head on an oar and prepared to die. That was when I saw Jaime Manjarrés, seated on the deck of the destroyer, pointing with his index finger toward port. Jaime Manjarrés, from Bogotá, is one of my oldest friends in the Navy. Often I thought of my mates who had tried to reach the raft. I wondered whether they had reached the other raft, whether the destroyer had picked them up or the planes had located them. But I had never thought of Jaime Manjarrés. Nonetheless, as soon as I closed my eyes he appeared, smiling, first pointing toward port, then sitting in the ship's mess, in front of me, holding a plate of fruit and scrambled eggs in his hand.

It was a dream at first. I would close my eyes and sleep for a few moments and Jaime Manjarrés would appear, at the same time and in the same place. Finally I decided to speak to him. I don't remember what I asked him that first time. I don't remember what he answered, either. But I know that we were talking on deck and suddenly there was the shock of the wave, the fatal wave of 11:55, and I woke up with a jolt, holding on with all my strength so I wouldn't fall into the ocean.

Just before dawn the sky darkened. I was too exhausted even to sleep. Surrounded by darkness, I gave up trying to see the other end of the raft. But I kept peering into the obscurity, attempting to penetrate it. That was when I clearly saw Jaime Manjarrés sitting on the gunwale, dressed in his uniform: blue pants and shirt, his cap slightly tilted over his right ear, on which I could clearly read, despite the darkness, "A.R.C. Caldas."

"Hello," I said to him, without a start.

Undoubtedly Jaime Manjarrés was there. Undoubtedly he had always been there.

If this had been a dream, it wouldn't have mattered. But I knew I was fully awake, completely lucid, and I could hear the whistling of the wind and the sounds of the sea. I felt hungry and thirsty. And I hadn't the slightest doubt that Jaime Manjarrés was with me on the raft.

"Why didn't you drink enough water on the ship?" he asked me.

"Because we were about to dock at Cartagena," I answered. "I was resting with Ramón Herrera on the stern deck."

It wasn't an apparition; I wasn't afraid. It seemed ridiculous that I had felt lonely before, not realizing that another sailor was on the raft.

"Why didn't you eat?" Jaime Manjarrés asked me. I clearly remember answering, "Because they didn't want to give me food. I asked them to give me apples and ice cream, but they didn't want to. I don't know where they were hiding the food."

Jaime Manjarrés didn't reply. He was silent for a moment. He turned to show me the way to Cartagena. I followed the direction in which he was pointing and saw the lights on shore and the buoys dancing in the harbor. "We're there," I said, continuing to look intently at the lights of the port, without emotion, without joy, as if I were arriving after a normal voyage. I asked Jaime Manjarrés if we could row a bit. But he was no longer there. I was alone in the raft, and the harbor lights became the rays of the sun. The first sunshine of my third day of solitude at sea.

6

A Rescue Ship and an Island of Cannibals

At first I kept track of the days by going over the dates. The first day, February 28, was the day of the accident. The second was the day of the planes. The third was the most difficult: nothing in particular happened. The raft moved along, propelled by the breeze. I had no strength to row. The day clouded over, I felt cold, and I lost my bearings because I couldn't see the sun. That morning I wouldn't have been able to guess where the planes had come from. A raft has no bow or stern; it's square and sometimes it floats sideways, imperceptibly turning around. Since there are no points of reference, you don't know whether it's moving forward or backward. The sea is the same in every direction. So I didn't know if the raft had changed course or if it had turned itself around. After the third day, something similar happened with time.

At midday I decided to do two things: First, I secured

an oar to one end of the raft, to find out if it always moved in the same direction. Second, using my keys, I made a scratch on the gunwale for each day that passed and marked the date. I made the first scratch and a number: 28. I made the second scratch and added the number 29. On the third day, next to the third scratch, I wrote the number 30. That was a mistake. I thought it was the thirtieth, but it was actually the second of March. I realized that only on the fourth day, when I wondered whether the month just ended was thirty or thirty-one days long. It was only then that I remembered it was February, and though it now seems like a trivial mistake, the error confused my sense of time. By the fourth day I wasn't very sure of my tally of the days I had spent on the raft. Was it three? Four? Five? According to my marks, no matter whether it was February or March, it was three days. But I wasn't very sure, just as I wasn't sure whether the raft was moving forward or backward. I preferred leaving things as they were to avoid further confusion. And I completely lost all hope that I would be rescued.

I still had not eaten or drunk anything. I didn't want to think anymore, because it took effort just to organize my thoughts. My skin, burned by the sun, hurt terribly and was covered with blisters. At the naval base the instructor had advised us to make certain, at all costs, not to let the lungs be exposed to the sun's rays. That was one of my worries. I had taken off my shirt, still wet, and tied it around my waist. Since I hadn't had any water for three days, it was now impossible to sweat. I felt a deep pain in my throat, in my chest, and beneath my shoulder blades, and so on the fourth day I drank a little sea water. It doesn't quench your thirst, but it's refreshing. I had held

off drinking it for so long because I knew that the second
time one should drink less, and only after many hours
had passed.

Every day at five, astonishingly punctual, the sharks
arrived. Then there was a banquet around the raft. Huge
fish would jump out of the water and, a few moments
later, resurface in pieces. The sharks, crazed, would silently
rush up to the bloody surface. So far, they hadn't tried to
smash the raft, but they were attracted to it because of its
white color. Everyone knows that sharks are more likely
to attack things that are white. Sharks are myopic and only
see white or shiny objects. Then I remembered another
of the instructor's recommendations: "Hide all shiny things
so as not to draw the sharks' attention."

I didn't have anything shiny—my watch is dark, even
its face. But I would have felt better if I had had white
things to throw overboard, away from the raft, in the event
the sharks tried to jump up over the edge. Just in case,
from the fourth day on, I held my oar poised after five each
evening, ready to defend myself.

A ship in sight

During the night I placed one oar across the raft and
tried to sleep. I don't know if it happened only when I was
asleep or also when I was awake, but I saw Jaime Manjarrés
every night. We chatted for a while, about everything, and
then he disappeared. I grew accustomed to his visits.

When the sun rose I thought I must have been hallucinating, but at night I hadn't the slightest doubt that Jaime
Manjarrés was there on board with me. He tried to go
to sleep, too, at dawn on the fifth day. He rested in

silence, with his head on the other oar. Soon he began searching the sea. He said, "Look!"

I looked up. About thirty kilometers from the raft, moving in the same direction as the wind, I saw the intermittent but unmistakable lights of a ship.

It had been hours since I had had the strength to row. But when I saw the lights I pulled myself together, grabbed the oars firmly, and tried to row toward the ship. I watched it slowly advance, and for an instant I saw not only the lights of the mast but also its shadow moving across the first light of dawn.

The wind put up stiff resistance. Even though I rowed furiously, with abnormal strength after four days without eating or sleeping, I don't think I managed to divert the raft even one meter from the direction in which the wind was blowing it.

The lights grew more distant, and I began to sweat. I was exhausted. After twenty minutes, the lights disappeared completely. The stars began to dim and the sky was tinted a deep gray. Desolate in the middle of the ocean, I let go of the oars, stood up, and, lashed by the icy wind of dawn, screamed like a lunatic for a few minutes.

When I saw the sun again, I was resting on the oar. I was completely spent. Now I saw no chance of being rescued and I began to want to die. But then I thought of something dangerous, and that thought strengthened my will to go on.

On the morning of my fifth day I was determined to change the course of the raft, by whatever means I could. It occurred to me that if I stayed on the course set by the wind, I would reach an island inhabited by cannibals. In Mobile, in a magazine whose name I've forgotten, I read a story about a shipwrecked sailor who was devoured by cannibals. But I was thinking more about *The Renegade*

Sailor, a book I had read in Bogotá two years earlier. This is the story of a sailor, during the war, who, after his ship collides with a mine, manages to swim to a nearby island. He stays there for twenty-four hours, eating wild fruit, until the cannibals discover him, throw him in a pot of boiling water, and cook him alive. The thought of that island lingered in my mind. Soon I couldn't think about the coastline without imagining a region populated by cannibals. For the first time in five days of solitude at sea, my terror was transformed: now I wasn't as afraid of the sea as I was of land.

At midday I rested on the gunwale, drowsy from the sun and hunger and thirst. I wasn't thinking about anything. I had no sense of time or of my course. I tried to stand up to test my strength and had the sensation that I couldn't move my body.

This is the moment, I thought. And in fact it seemed to be the most dreadful moment of all, the one the instructor had described to us: when you lash yourself to the raft. There is an instant in which you feel neither thirst nor hunger, in which you don't even feel the relentless bite of the sun on your blistered skin. You don't think. You have no sense of what your feelings are. But still you don't lose hope. There is still the last recourse of loosening the ropes of the mesh floor and lashing yourself to the raft. During the war many corpses were found like that, decomposed and pecked by birds, yet firmly tied to the raft.

I thought I still had the strength to wait until nightfall before tying myself up. I rolled myself into the bottom of the raft, stretched out my legs, and remained submerged up to my neck for a few hours. When the sun touched the wound on my knee it began to hurt. It was as if it had been awakened. And as if the pain had given me a new desire to live. Little by little, in the cool water I began to recover my strength. Then I felt a wrenching twist in my stomach and my bowels moved, shaken by a long, deep rumble. I tried to hold out but I couldn't.

With great difficulty I sat up, undid my belt, lowered my pants, and mercifully relieved myself for the first time in five days. And for the first time the fish, desperate, charged the side of the raft, trying to rip through the thick rope mesh.

Seven sea gulls

The sight of fish, glistening and close by, made me hungry again. For the first time I felt truly desperate. But at the very least, I had some bait. I forgot my exhaustion, grabbed an oar, and prepared to expend the last of my strength in a well-aimed blow to the head of one of the frenzied fish that were jumping at the side of the raft. I don't know how many times I swung the oar. It felt as if each blow had hit the mark, but I waited in vain for my catch. There was a terrible feast of fish devouring one another, with one shark, belly up, taking his succulent share from the turbulent water.

The shark's presence diverted me from my intentions; discouraged, I lay down at the side of the raft. But after a few moments I was filled with glee; seven sea gulls flew over the raft.

To a hungry sailor alone at sea, gulls are a message of hope. Ordinarily, a flock of sea gulls will accompany a ship out of port, but only up to the second day of the voyage. Seven sea gulls over the raft meant land was nearby.

If I had had the strength, I would have started to row. But I was too weak. I could barely stay on my feet for a few seconds at a time. Convinced that I was less than two days from land, I drank a little more sea water from the palm of my hand and again lay down at the side of the raft, face upward so the sun wouldn't burn my lungs. I didn't cover my face with my shirt because I wanted to go on looking at the sea gulls, which were flying slowly, swooping down at an acute angle to the sea. It was one o'clock in the afternoon on the fifth day.

I don't know when it arrived. I was lying down in the raft, around five in the afternoon, preparing to lower myself into the middle before the sharks came. Then I saw a small sea gull, about the size of my hand, fly in circles above the raft and land on the end opposite me.

My mouth filled with icy saliva. I didn't have anything to capture that sea gull with. No instrument except my hands and my cunning, which was sharpened by hunger. The other gulls had disappeared. Only this little one remained, brown, with shiny feathers, hopping around on the gunwale.

I kept absolutely still. I thought I felt, against my shoulder, the sharp fin of the punctual shark, who would have arrived at five o'clock. But I decided to take a risk. I didn't dare look at the sea gull, so as not to scare it off by moving my head. I watched it fly very low over my body. I saw it take to the air and disappear into the sky. But I didn't lose hope. I was hungry and I knew that if I remained absolutely still the sea gull would come within reach of my hand.

I waited more than half an hour, I think. It came and went several times. At one point I felt a fin brush past my head as a shark tore a fish to pieces. But I was more hungry than frightened. The sea gull jumped around on the edge of the raft. It was twilight on my fifth day at sea: five days without eating. Despite my emotion, despite my heart pounding in my chest, I kept completely still, like a dead man, while I waited for the sea gull to come closer.

I was stretched out on my back at the side of the raft with my hands on my thighs. I'm sure that for half an hour I didn't dare to blink. The sky brightened and irritated my eyes, but I didn't close them at that tense moment. The sea gull pecked at my shoes.

After another long, intense half hour had passed I felt the sea gull sit on my leg. It pecked softly at my pants. I kept perfectly still when it gave me a sharp, dry peck on the knee, though I could have leaped into the air from the pain of the knee wound. But I endured it. Then the sea gull wandered to my right thigh, five or six centimeters from my hand. I stopped breathing and, desperately tense, began imperceptibly to slide my hand toward it.

7

The Desperate Recourse
of a Starving Man

If you lie down in a village square hoping to capture a
sea gull, you could stay there your whole life without
succeeding. But a hundred miles from shore it's different.
Sea gulls have a highly developed instinct for self-
preservation on land but at sea they're very cocky.

I lay so still that the playful little sea gull perching
on my thigh probably thought I was dead. I watched it. It
pecked at my pants but didn't hurt me. I continued to
extend my hand. Suddenly, at the precise moment the sea
gull realized it was in danger and tried to take flight, I
grabbed it by the wing, leaped to the middle of the raft,
and prepared to devour it.

When I first hoped it would perch on my thigh, I was
sure that if I captured it I would eat it alive, without stop-
ping to pluck its feathers. I was starving, and even the
thought of the bird's blood made me thirsty. But once I

had it in my hands and felt the pulsing of its warm body and looked into its shiny, round dark-gray eyes, I hesitated.

Once, I had stood on deck with a rifle, trying to shoot one of the sea gulls following the ship, and the destroyer's gunnery officer, an experienced sailor, said, "Don't be a scoundrel. To a sailor, sea gulls are like sighting land. It isn't proper for a sailor to kill a sea gull." I remembered that incident, and the gunnery officer's words, as I held the captured sea gull in my hands, ready to kill it and tear it apart. Even though I hadn't eaten in five days, those words echoed in my ear, as if I were hearing them all over again. But hunger was more powerful than anything else. I grabbed the bird's head firmly and began to wring its neck, as you would a chicken's.

It was terribly delicate. With the first twist, I felt the neck bones break. With the second, I felt its living, warm blood spurt through my fingers. I pitied it. It looked like a murder victim. Its head, still pulsating, hung down from its body and throbbed in my hand.

The spilled blood stirred up the fish. The gleaming white belly of a shark grazed the side of the raft. A shark crazed by the scent of blood can bite through a sheet of steel. Since its jaws are on the underside of its body, it has to turn over to eat. But because it's myopic and greedy, when it turns belly up it drags along everything in its path. I think one of the sharks tried to attack the raft. Terrified, I threw the sea gull's head at it and watched, only centimeters from the raft, the great struggle of those huge beasts over that morsel which was even smaller than an egg.

The bird was extremely light and the bones were so fragile you could crush them with your fingers. I tried to pull the feathers off, but they adhered to the delicate white skin and the flesh came away with the bloody feathers. The viscous black liquid on my fingers disgusted me.

It's easy to say that after five days of hunger you can eat anything. But though you may be starving, you still feel nauseated by a mess of warm, bloody feathers with a strong odor of raw fish and of mange.

At first I tried to pluck the feathers carefully, methodically. But I hadn't counted on the fragility of the skin. As the feathers came out it began to disintegrate in my hands. I washed the bird in the middle of the raft. I pulled it apart with a single jerk, and the sight of the pink intestines and blue veins turned my stomach. I put a sliver of the thigh in my mouth but I couldn't swallow it. This was absurd. It was like chewing on a frog. Unable to get over my repugnance, I spit out the piece of flesh and kept still for a long time, with the revolting hash of bloody feathers and bones in my hand.

The first thing that occurred to me was that whatever I couldn't eat might serve as bait. But I didn't have a single implement for fishing. I should have had at least a pin or a bit of wire. But I had nothing, apart from keys, watch, ring, and the three business cards from the shop in Mobile.

I considered my belt. Perhaps I might be able to fashion a fishhook from the buckle. But my efforts were useless. It was growing dark and the fish were leaping all around the raft, crazed at the scent of blood. When it was completely dark I flung the remains of the sea gull overboard and lay down to sleep. As I arranged the oar, I imagined the silent battle of fish fighting over the bones I couldn't bring myself to eat.

I think I could have died of exhaustion and hopelessness

that night. A harsh wind came up during the early hours. The raft pitched and rolled while—not even remembering now to take the precaution of lashing myself to the mesh flooring—I lay exhausted in the bottom of the raft, with my head and feet barely above water.

But after midnight there was a change: the moon appeared, for the first time since the accident. Beneath the clear blue night, the surface of the sea once again took on a spectral look. That night Jaime Manjarrés didn't appear. I was alone, without hope, and resigned to my fate.

Nevertheless, each time my spirits sank, something would happen to renew my hopes. That night it was the reflection of the moon on the waves. The sea was choppy and in each wave I thought I saw the lights of a ship. Two nights before, I had lost hope that a ship would rescue me. But all through that night illumined by the moon—my sixth night at sea—I searched the horizon desperately, almost as intently and hopefully as I had on the first night. If I found myself in the same predicament today, I would die of hopelessness: I now know that no ship travels the course on which my raft was bound.

I was a dead man

I don't remember the dawn of the next day. I have a vague idea that during the entire morning I lay prostrate, between life and death, in the bottom of the raft. I thought about my family and imagined them doing precisely what they later told me they had done during my disappearance. I wasn't surprised when they said they had held a wake for me. On that sixth morning of solitude at sea, I guessed that all those things were happening. I knew that my family had been informed of my disappearance. Since the planes hadn't come back, I was sure they had abandoned the search and declared me dead.

All of that was so, up to a point. Yet I tried to take care of myself every moment. I kept finding ways to survive, something to prop myself up with—insignificant though it might have been—some reason to sustain hope. But on the sixth day I no longer hoped for anything. I was a dead man in the raft.

In the afternoon, thinking about how soon five o'clock would come, and with it the return of the sharks, I tried to lash myself to the side. On the beach in Cartagena two years earlier I had seen the remains of a man who had been mangled by a shark. I didn't want to die that way. I didn't want to be torn to shreds by a mob of voracious beasts.

It was almost five. The sharks arrived and circled the raft. I struggled to rouse myself to untie a rope from the mesh floor. The afternoon was cool, the sea calm. I felt slightly stronger. Suddenly I saw the sea gulls from the previous day, and the sight of them reawakened my desire to live.

At that point I would have eaten anything. Hunger gnawed at me. But the pain in my ravaged throat and in my jaws, hardened by lack of exercise, was worse. I needed to chew something. I tried in vain to tear off pieces of the rubber sole of my shoe. Then I remembered the business cards from the shop in Mobile.

They were in one of my pants pockets, nearly disintegrated from the dampness. I tore them up, put them in my mouth, and began to chew. It was like a miracle: my throat felt a little better and my mouth filled with saliva. I chewed slowly, as if it were gum. My jaws hurt at the first

bite. But eventually, chewing the cards I had saved without knowing why since the day I went shopping with
Mary Address, I felt stronger and more optimistic. I
thought I would keep chewing them forever to relieve the
pain in my jaw. It seemed terribly wasteful to throw them
overboard. I could feel a tiny piece of mashed-up card-
board move all the way down to my stomach, and from
that moment on I felt I would be saved, that I wouldn't be
destroyed by the sharks.

What do shoes taste like?

The relief I felt while chewing the cards spurred my
imagination to look for things to eat. If I had had a knife,
I would have cut up my shoes and chewed slices of the
rubber soles. They were the closest thing at hand. I tried
to pry off the clean, white soles with my keys. But I
couldn't pull off a piece of the sole, it was glued so tightly
to the fabric.

Desperately I gnawed at my belt until my teeth hurt. I
couldn't even tear off a mouthful. I must have looked like
a fiend then, trying to rip off pieces of my shoes, belt, and
shirt with my teeth. At twilight I took off my clothes,
which were now soaked with sweat, and I was down to my
shorts. I don't know if it was the result of chewing the cards,
but I fell asleep almost immediately. Perhaps because I had
grown accustomed to the discomfort of the raft, perhaps
because I was so drained after six nights of keeping a vigil, I
slept soundly for many hours. At times a wave would
awaken me. I would start up, frightened that the force of
the wave would throw me into the water, but immediately
afterward I would go back to sleep.

Eventually I woke to my seventh day at sea. I don't know why I was sure it wouldn't be my last. The sea was calm and the day cloudy, and when, at about eight o'clock, the sun came out, I felt reassured by the good sleep of the previous night. Against the low, leaden sky, the seven sea gulls flew over the raft.

Two days before, I had been cheered by their presence. But when I saw them the third time, I felt terror again. They're seven lost sea gulls, I thought in despair. Every sailor knows that sea gulls sometimes get lost at sea and fly for several days without direction, until they find a ship to point the way to port. Maybe the gulls I had been seeing for three days now were the same ones each day, lost at sea. That meant my raft was drifting farther and farther from land.

8

Fighting Off the Sharks for a Fish

The thought that for seven days I had been drifting farther out to sea rather than nearing land crushed my resolve to keep on struggling. But when you feel close to death, your instinct for self-preservation grows stronger. For several reasons, that day was very different from the previous days: the sea was dark and calm; the sun, warm and tranquil, hugged my body; a gentle breeze guided the raft along; even my sunburn felt a bit better.

The fish were different, too. From very early on they had escorted the raft, swimming near the surface. And I could see them clearly: blue fish, gray-brown ones, red ones. There were fish of every color, all shapes and sizes. It seemed as if the raft were floating in an aquarium.

I don't know whether, after seven days without food and adrift at sea, one becomes accustomed to living that way. I think so. The hopelessness of the previous day was replaced by a mellow resignation devoid of emotion. I was

sure that everything was different, that the sea and the
sky were no longer hostile, and that the fish accompanying
me on my journey were my friends. My old acquaintances
of seven days.

That morning I wasn't thinking about reaching any
destination. I was certain that the raft had arrived in a
region where there were no ships, where even sea gulls
could go astray.

I thought, however, that after seven days adrift I would
become accustomed to the sea, to my anxious way of life,
without having to spur my imagination in order to survive.
After all, I had endured a week of harsh winds and waves.
Why wouldn't it be possible to live on the raft indefinitely?
The fish swam near the surface; the sea was clear and calm.
There were so many lovely, tempting fish around the raft
it looked as if I could grab them with my hands. Not a
shark was in sight. Confidently I put my hand in the water
and tried to seize a round fish, a bright blue one about
twenty centimeters long. It was as if I had flung a stone:
all the fish fled instantly, momentarily churning up the
water. Then slowly they came back to the surface.

You have to be crafty to fish with your hand, I thought.
Underwater, the hand didn't have as much strength or
agility. I chose one fish from the bunch. I tried to grab it.
And in fact I did. But I felt it slip through my fingers
with disconcerting speed and nimbleness. I waited patiently, not pressuring myself, just trying to catch a fish.
I wasn't thinking about the shark which might be out
there, waiting until I put my arm in up to the elbow so
he could make off with it in one sure bite. I kept busy
trying to catch fish until a little after ten o'clock. But it
was useless. They nibbled at my fingers, gently at first, as

when they nibble at bait. Then a little harder. A smooth silver fish about a foot and a half long, with minute, sharp teeth, tore the skin off my thumb. Then I realized that the nibbles of the other fish hadn't been harmless: all my fingers had small bleeding cuts.

Shark in the raft!

I don't know if it was the blood from my fingers, but in an instant there was a riot of sharks around the raft. I had never seen so many. I had never seen them so voracious. They leaped like dolphins, chasing the fish and devouring them. Terrified, I sat in the middle of the raft and watched the massacre.

The next thing happened so quickly that I didn't realize just when it was that the shark leaped out of the water, thrashing its tail violently, and the raft, tottering, sank beneath the gleaming foam. In the midst of the huge, glittering wave that crashed over the side there was a metallic flash. Instinctively I grabbed an oar and prepared to strike a deathblow. But then I saw the enormous fin, and I realized what had happened. Chased by the shark, a brilliant green fish, almost half a meter long, had leaped into the raft. With all my strength I walloped it on the head with my oar.

Killing a fish inside a raft isn't easy. The vessel tottered with each blow; it might have turned over. It was a perilous moment. I needed all my strength and all my wits about me. If I struck out blindly, the raft would turn over and I would plunge into a sea full of hungry sharks. If I didn't aim carefully, my quarry would escape. I stood between life and death. I would either end up in the gullet of a shark or get four pounds of fresh fish to appease the hunger of seven days.

I braced myself on the gunwale and struck the second blow. I felt the wooden oar drive into the fish's skull. The raft bounced. The sharks shuddered below. I pressed myself firmly against the side. When the raft stabilized, the fish was still alive.

In agony, a fish can jump higher and farther than it otherwise can. I knew the third blow had to be a sure one or I would lose my prey forever.

After a lunge at the fish, I found myself sitting on the floor, where I thought I had a better chance of grabbing it. If necessary, I would have captured it with my feet, between my knees, or in my teeth. I anchored myself to the floor. Trying not to make a mistake and convinced that my life depended on my next blow, I swung the oar with all my strength. The fish stopped moving and a thread of dark blood tinted the water inside the raft.

I could smell the blood, and the sharks sensed it, too. Suddenly, with four pounds of fish within my grasp, I felt uncontrollable terror: driven wild by the scent of blood, the sharks hurled themselves with all their strength against the bottom of the raft. The raft shook. I realized that it could turn over in an instant. I could be torn to pieces by the three rows of steel teeth in the jaws of each shark.

But the pressure of hunger was greater than anything else. I squeezed the fish between my legs and, staggering, began the difficult job of balancing the raft each time it suffered another assault by the sharks. That went on for several minutes. Whenever the raft stabilized, I threw the bloody water overboard. Little by little the water cleared and the beasts calmed down. But I had to be careful: a

terrifyingly huge shark fin—the biggest I had ever seen—
protruded more than a meter above the water's surface.
The shark was swimming peacefully, but I knew that if it
caught the scent of blood it would give a shudder that
could capsize the raft. With extreme caution I began to
try to pull my fish apart.

A creature that's half a meter long is protected by a
hard crust of scales: if you try to pull them off, you find
that they adhere to the flesh like armor plating. I had no
sharp instruments. I tried to shave off the scales with my
keys, but they wouldn't budge. Meanwhile, it occurred to
me that I had never seen a fish like this one: it was deep
green and thickly scaled. From when I was little, I had
associated the color green with poison. Incredibly, although
my stomach was throbbing painfully at the prospect of even
a mouthful of fresh fish, I had trouble deciding whether
or not that strange creature might be poisonous.

My poor body

Hunger is bearable when you have no hope of food. But
it was never so insistent as when I was trying to slash that
shiny green flesh with my keys.

After a few minutes, I realized I would have to use more
violent methods if I wanted to eat my victim. I stood up,
stepped hard on its tail, and stuck the oar handle into one
of its gills. I saw that the fish wasn't dead yet. I hit it on
the head again. Then I tried to tear off the hard protective
plates that covered the gills. I couldn't tell whether the
blood streaming over my fingers was from the fish or from
me; my hands were covered with wounds and my fingertips were raw.

The scent of blood once again stirred the sharks' hunger. It seems unbelievable but, furious at the hungry beasts and disgusted by the sight of the bloody fish, I was on the point of throwing it to the sharks, as I had done with the sea gull. I felt utterly frustrated and helpless at the sight of the solid, impenetrable body of the fish.

I examined it meticulously for soft spots. Finally I found a slit between the gills and with my finger I began to pull out the entrails. The innards of a fish are soft and without substance. It is said that if you strike a hard blow to a shark's tail the stomach and intestines fall out of its mouth. In Cartagena, I had seen sharks hanging by their tails, with huge thick masses of dark innards oozing from their mouths.

Luckily the entrails of my fish were as soft as those of the sharks. It didn't take long to remove them with my finger. It was a female: among the entrails I found a string of eggs. When it was completely gutted I took the first bite. I couldn't break through the crust of scales. But on the second try, with renewed strength, I bit down desperately, until my jaw ached. Then I managed to tear off the first mouthful and began to chew the cold, tough flesh.

I chewed with disgust. I had always found the odor of raw fish repulsive, but the flavor is even more repugnant. It tastes vaguely like raw palm, but oilier and less palatable. I couldn't imagine that anyone had ever eaten a live fish, but as I chewed the first food that had reached my lips in seven days, I had the awful certainty that I was in fact eating one.

After the first piece, I felt better immediately. I took a second bite and chewed again. A moment before, I had thought I could eat a whole shark. But now I felt full after the second mouthful. The terrible hunger of seven days was appeased in an instant. I was strong again, as on the first day.

I now know that raw fish slakes your thirst. I hadn't known it before, but I realized that the fish had appeased not only my hunger but my thirst as well. I was sated and optimistic. I still had food for a long time, since I had taken only two small bites of a creature half a meter long.

I decided to wrap the fish in my shirt and store it in the bottom of the raft to keep it fresh. But first I had to wash it. Absentmindedly I held it by the tail and dunked it once over the side. But blood had coagulated between the scales. It would have to be scrubbed. Naïvely I submerged it again. And that was when I felt the charge of the violent thrust of the shark's jaws. I hung on to the tail of the fish with all the strength I had. The beast's lunge upset my balance. I was thrown against the side of the raft but I held on to my food supply; I clung to it like a savage. In that fraction of a second, it didn't occur to me that with another bite the shark could have ripped my arm off at the shoulder. I kept pulling with all my strength, but now there was nothing in my hands. The shark had made off with my prey. Infuriated, rabid with frustration, I grabbed an oar and delivered a tremendous blow to the shark's head when it passed by the side of the raft. The beast leaped; it twisted furiously and with one clean, savage bite splintered the oar and swallowed half of it.

9

The Color of the Sea Begins to Change

In a rage, I continued to strike at the water with the broken oar. I had to avenge myself on the shark that had snatched from my hand the only nourishment available. It was almost five in the afternoon of my seventh day at sea. Soon the sharks would arrive en masse. I felt strengthened by the two bites I had managed to eat, and the fury occasioned by the loss of my fish made me want to fight. There were two more oars in the raft. I thought of switching the oar the shark had bitten off for another one, so I could keep battling the monsters. But my instinct for self-preservation was stronger than my rage: I realized I might lose the other two oars and I didn't know when I might need them.

Nightfall was the same as on all the other days, but this night was darker and the sea was stormy. It looked like rain. Thinking some drinking water might be coming my way, I took off my shoes and my shirt to have something in which to catch it. It was what landlubbers call a night that isn't fit for a dog. At sea, it should be called a night that isn't fit for a shark.

After nine, an icy wind began to blow. I tried to escape it by lying in the bottom of the raft, but that didn't work. The chill penetrated to the marrow of my bones. I had to put my shirt and shoes back on and resign myself to the fact that the rain would take me by surprise and I wouldn't have anything to collect it in. The waves were more powerful than they'd been on February 28, the day of the accident. The raft was like an eggshell on the choppy, dirty sea. I couldn't sleep. I had submerged myself in the raft up to my neck because the wind was even icier than the water was. I kept shuddering. At one point I thought I could no longer endure the cold and I tried doing exercises to warm up. But I was too weak. I had to cling tightly to the side to keep from being thrown into the sea by the powerful waves. I rested my head on the oar that had been demolished by the shark. The others lay at the bottom of the raft.

Before midnight the gale got worse, the sky grew dense and turned a deep gray, the air became more humid, and not a single drop of rain fell. But just after midnight an enormous wave—as big as the one that had swept over the deck of the destroyer—lifted the raft like a banana peel, upended it, and in a fraction of a second turned it upside down.

I only realized what had happened when I found myself in the water, swimming toward the surface as I had on the afternoon of the accident. I swam frantically, reached the surface, and then thought I would die of shock: I could not see the raft. I saw the enormous black waves over my head and I remembered Luis Rengifo—strong, a good swimmer, well fed—who hadn't been able to reach the raft from only two meters away. I had become disoriented and was looking in the wrong direction. But behind me, about a meter away, the raft appeared, battered by the waves. I reached it in two strokes. You can swim two strokes in two seconds, but those two seconds can feel like eternity. I was so terrified that in one leap I found myself panting and dripping in the bottom of the raft. My heart was throbbing in my chest and I couldn't breathe.

My lucky star

I had no quarrel with my luck. If the raft had overturned at five o'clock in the evening, the sharks would have torn me to pieces. But at midnight they're quiet. And even more so when the sea is stirred up.

When I sat down in the raft again, I was clutching the oar that the shark had demolished. Everything had happened so quickly that all my movements had been instinctive. Later I remembered that when I fell in the water the oar hit my head and I grabbed it when I began to sink. It was the only oar left on the raft. The others had disappeared.

So as not to lose even this small stick, half destroyed by the shark, I tied it securely with a loose rope from the mesh flooring. The sea was still raging. This time I had been lucky. If the raft overturned again, I might not be able to reach it. With that in mind, I undid my belt and lashed myself to the mesh floor.

The waves crashed over the side. The raft danced on the turbulent sea, but I was secure, tied to the ropes by my belt. The oar was also secure. As I worked to ensure that the raft wouldn't overturn again, I realized I had nearly lost my shirt and shoes. If I hadn't been so cold, they would have been at the bottom of the raft, together with the other two oars, when it overturned.

It's perfectly normal for a raft to overturn in rough seas. The vessel is made of cork and covered with waterproof fabric painted white. But the bottom isn't rigid; it hangs from the cork frame like a basket. If the raft turns over in the water, the bottom immediately returns to its normal position. The only danger is in losing the raft. For that reason, I figured that as long as I was tied to it, the raft could turn over a thousand times without my losing it.

That was a fact. But there was one thing I hadn't foreseen. A quarter of an hour after the first one, the raft did a second spectacular somersault. First I was suspended in the icy, damp air, whipped by the gale. Then I saw hell right before my eyes: I realized which way the raft would turn over. I tried to move to the opposite side to provide equilibrium, but I was bound to the ropes by the thick leather belt. Instantly I realized what was happening: the raft had overturned completely. I was at the bottom, lashed firmly to the rope webbing. I was drowning; my hands searched frantically for the belt buckle to open it.

Panic-stricken but trying not to become confused, I thought how to undo the buckle. I knew I hadn't wasted much time: in good physical condition I could stay underwater more than eighty seconds. As soon as I had found myself under the raft, I had stopped breathing. That was at least five seconds gone. I ran my hand around my waist and in less than a second, I think, I found the belt. In another second I found the buckle. It was fastened to the ropes in such a way that I had to push myself away from the raft with my other hand to release it. I wasted time looking for a place to grab hold. Then I pushed off with my left hand. My right hand grasped the buckle, oriented itself quickly, and loosened the belt. Keeping the buckle open, I lowered my body toward the bottom, without letting go of the side, and in a fraction of a second I was free of the ropes. I felt my lungs gasping for breath. With one last effort, I grabbed the side with both hands and pulled with all my strength, still not breathing. Bringing my full weight to bear on it, I succeeded in turning the raft over again. But I was still underneath it.

I was swallowing water. My throat, ravaged by thirst, burned terribly. But I barely noticed. The important thing was not to let go of the raft. I managed to raise my head to the surface. I breathed. I was so tired. I didn't think I had the strength to lift myself over the side. But I was terrified to be in the same water that had been infested with sharks only hours before. Absolutely certain it would be the final effort of my life, I called on my last reserves of energy, leaped over the side, and fell exhausted into the bottom of the raft.

I don't know how long I lay there, face up, with my throat burning and my raw fingertips throbbing. But I do know I was concerned with only two things: that my lungs quiet down and that the raft not turn over again.

The sun at daybreak

That was how my eighth day at sea dawned. The morning was stormy. If it had rained, I wouldn't have had the strength to collect drinking water. I thought rain would revive me, but not a drop fell, even though the humidity in the air was like an announcement of imminent rain. The sea was still choppy at daybreak. It didn't calm down until after eight, but then the sun came out and the sky turned an intense blue again.

Completely spent, I lay down at the side of the raft and took a few swallows of sea water. I now know that it's not harmful to the body. But I didn't know it then, and I only resorted to it when the pain in my throat became unbearable. After seven days at sea, thirst is a feeling unto itself; it's a deep pain in the throat, in the sternum, and especially beneath the clavicles. And it's also the fear of suffocating. The sea water relieved the pain.

After a storm the sea turns blue, as in pictures. Near the shore, tree trunks and roots torn up by the storm float gently along. Gulls emerge to fly over the water. That morning, when the breeze died down, the surface of the water turned metallic and the raft glided along in a straight line. The warm wind felt reassuring to my body and my spirit.

A big old dark gull flew over the raft. I had no doubt then that I was near land. The sea gull I had captured a few days earlier was a young bird. At that age they can fly great distances—they can be found many miles into the interior. But an old sea gull, big and heavy like the one I had just seen, couldn't fly a hundred miles from shore.

I felt renewed strength. As I had done on the first days, I began to search the horizon again. Vast numbers of sea gulls came from every direction.

I had company and I was happy. I wasn't hungry. More and more frequently I took drinks of sea water. I wasn't lonely in the midst of the immense number of sea gulls circling over my head. I remembered Mary Address. What had become of her? I wondered, remembering her voice when she translated the dialogue for me at the movies. In fact, on that day—the only one on which I had thought of Mary Address for no reason at all, and surely not because the sky was full of sea gulls—Mary was at a Catholic church in Mobile hearing a mass for the eternal rest of my soul. That mass, as Mary later wrote to me in Cartagena, was celebrated on the eighth day of my disappearance. It was for the repose of my soul, but I now think it was also for the repose of my body, for that morning, while I thought about Mary Address and she attended mass in Mobile, I was happy at sea, watching the sea gulls that proved land was near.

I spent almost all day sitting on the side of the raft, searching the horizon. The day was startlingly clear, and I was certain I saw land once from a distance of fifty miles. The raft had assumed a speed that two men with oars couldn't have equaled. It moved in a straight line, as if propelled by a motor along the calm, blue surface.

After spending seven days on a raft one can detect the slightest change in the color of the water. On March 7, at three-thirty in the afternoon, I noticed that the raft had reached an area where the water wasn't blue, but dark green. There was a definite demarcation: on one side was the blue water I had been seeing for seven days; on the other, green water that looked denser. The sky was full of

sea gulls flying very low. I could hear them flapping over
my head. The signs were unmistakable: the change in the
color of the water and the abundance of sea gulls told me
I should keep a vigil that night, alert for the first lights of
shore.

IO

Hope Abandoned . . . Until Death

I didn't have to force myself to go to sleep on my eighth night at sea. At nine o'clock the old sea gull perched on the side of the raft and stayed there all night long. I lay down against the only remaining oar. The night was calm and the raft moved forward in a straight line toward a definite point. Where am I going? I asked myself, convinced by all the signs—the color of the ocean, the old sea gull—that I would be ashore the next day. I hadn't the slightest idea where the raft was headed, driven by the wind.

I wasn't sure whether the raft had stayed on its original course. If it had followed the route the planes flew, it was likely to end up in Colombia. But without a compass it was impossible to know. If it had traveled south in a straight line, it would undoubtedly land on the Caribbean coast of Colombia. But it was also possible that it had traveled northward. If that was the case, I had no idea of my position at all.

Before midnight, as I was beginning to fall asleep, the old sea gull came over and pecked me on the head. It didn't hurt. The bird pecked me gently, without injuring my scalp. It seemed as if it were caressing me. I remembered the gunnery officer on the destroyer who had told me it was undignified for a sailor to kill a sea gull, and I felt remorseful about the little one that I had killed for no good reason.

I searched the horizon until dawn. It wasn't cold that night. But I saw no lights. There was no sign of the coastline. The raft slipped along on a clear, calm sea, but all around me there were no lights other than the stars. When I remained completely still, the sea gull seemed to be asleep. It lowered its head as it perched on the side and kept perfectly motionless for a long time. But as soon as I moved, it gave a little start and pecked my head.

At dawn I changed position, so that the sea gull was now at my feet. Then I felt it peck my shoes. It moved along the gunwale. I kept still; the sea gull also kept still. Then it perched on my head, still not moving. But as soon as I moved my head, it began to peck my hair, almost tenderly. It became a game. I changed position several times. And each time, the sea gull moved to where my head was. At daybreak, without having to move cautiously, I reached out and grabbed it by the neck.

I had no intention of killing it. My experience with the other sea gull proved that it would be a useless sacrifice. I was hungry, but I gave no thought to appeasing my hunger with that friendly bird, who had accompanied me all through the night and had done me no harm. When I grabbed it, it stretched its wings, shook itself briskly, and tried to free itself. Quickly I folded its wings across its neck, to prevent it from moving. Then it raised its head and in the first light of morning I saw its eyes, transparent and fearful. Even if I had had any thought of dismembering it, I would have changed my mind when I saw its enormous sad eyes.

The sun rose early and was so strong that the air was boiling by seven o'clock. I was still lying down, clutching the gull tightly. The sea was still dense and green as on the previous day, but there was no sign of shore in any direction. The air was suffocating, so I let go of my prisoner. The gull shook its head and took off like a shot into the sky. A moment later it rejoined the flock.

The sun that morning was much harsher than it had been all the other days. Although I had taken care not to let my lungs be exposed to it, my whole back was blistered. I had to remove the oar on which I had been resting and submerge myself because I could no longer bear the wood touching my back. My shoulders and arms were seared. I couldn't even touch the skin with my fingers because they felt like red-hot coals. My eyes burned. I couldn't focus on anything because the air would fill with blinding bright circles. Until that day I had not realized the sorry state I was in. I was worn out, blistered by the salt and the sun. With no effort at all I pulled large sheets of skin off my arms; underneath there was a smooth red surface. A moment later I felt a painful throbbing of the bare patch, and blood spurted through the pores.

I hadn't noticed my beard. I hadn't shaved in eleven days. A thick beard grew down to my throat, but I couldn't touch it because the skin, irritated by the sun, hurt terribly.

The thought of my emaciated face and wounded body reminded me of all I had suffered during those days of solitude and desperation. And again I despaired. There was no sign of the coast. It was midday and I had lost all hope of reaching land. Even if the raft covered a great distance, it couldn't possibly reach shore by twilight if I hadn't seen the coastline by now.

"*I want to die*"

A sense of happiness that had taken twelve hours to develop disappeared without a trace in one minute. My strength ebbed. I ceased all effort. For the first time in nine days I slept face down, with my burning back exposed to the sun. I did it without pity for my body. I knew that if I stayed that way until nightfall I would die.

At some point, you no longer feel pain. Sensation disappears and reason is dulled, until you lose all grasp of time and place. Face down in the raft, with my arms resting on the gunwale and my beard on my arms, I felt the sun's merciless bite. For hours the air was filled with luminous spots. Finally exhausted, I closed my eyes, but then the sun no longer burned my body. I was neither hungry nor thirsty. I felt nothing, other than complete indifference to life or death. I thought I was dying. And that thought filled me with a strange, dim hope.

When I opened my eyes again, I was in Mobile. It was suffocatingly hot and I had gone to a party at an outdoor café with some of my shipmates and Massey Nasser, the Jewish clerk in a shop in Mobile where we sailors bought clothing. He was the one who had given us the business

cards. During the eight months the ship was undergoing
repairs, Massey Nasser had made a point of taking care of
us Colombian sailors, and out of gratitude we did business
only with him. He spoke proper Spanish despite the fact
that, he told us, he had never lived in a Spanish-speaking
country.

At the outdoor café, where we went almost every Saturday, there were only Jews and Colombian sailors. Every
Saturday the same woman danced on a platform. Her
belly was bare and her face was veiled, like the Arab
dancers in films. We applauded and drank beer out of cans.
The most animated of us all was Massey Nasser, the Jewish
shop clerk who sold fine, cheap clothing to the Colombian
sailors.

I don't know how long I stayed like that, in a daze,
hallucinating about the party in Mobile. I only know that
I jumped up, thinking it was getting late. Then I saw,
about five meters from the raft, an enormous yellow turtle
with a striped head and impassive, motionless eyes, like
two giant crystal balls, gazing at me spookily. First I
thought I was hallucinating again, so I sat down, terrified.
The monstrous animal, about four meters long from head
to tail, submerged itself when it saw me move, leaving a
wake of foam. I didn't know if it was real or a fantasy.
And even now I can't decide if it was real, though for a
few minutes I saw that giant yellow turtle swimming ahead
of the raft, with its nightmarish painted head raised above
the water. I only know that—whether real or a fantasy—
if the turtle had even grazed the raft, that would have been
enough to cause it to turn over and spin around and around
a few times.

That terrible vision rekindled my fear. But fear revived

me. I grabbed the stunted oar, sat down, and prepared for battle, with this monster or any other that might try to overturn the raft. It was almost five. Punctual as always, the sharks came to the surface.

I looked at the side of the raft where I had marked each day and counted eight scratches. But I realized I had forgotten to record this one. I made a scratch with my key, convinced it would be the last one, feeling desperate and angry at the realization that it would be harder for me to die than to go on living. That morning I had chosen death but nonetheless continued to live, with the fragment of oar in my hand, ready to fight for life—to go on fighting for the only thing that didn't matter at all to me now.

The mysterious root

In the midst of the metallic sun and the despair and the thirst, which for the first time was becoming intolerable, something incredible happened. In the middle of the raft, tangled in the webbing, there was a red root like the ones that they crush in Boyacá to make dye, the name of which I can't remember. I didn't know how long it had been there. During the nine days at sea I hadn't even seen a blade of grass. Nonetheless, without my knowing how it had happened, the root was there, tangled in the ropes of the mesh floor, another unmistakable sign of land, which was, however, nowhere to be seen.

The root was about thirty centimeters long. Starving, but now without the strength even to think about hunger, I carelessly bit into it. It tasted like blood. But it exuded a thick, sweet oil that soothed my throat. I thought it tasted like poison, but I kept on eating it, devouring the gnarled stick until there wasn't a splinter left.

After I finished eating I didn't feel any better. It occurred to me that the root might have been an olive branch, because I remembered the Bible story: When Noah released the dove, it returned to the ark with an olive branch, a sign that the sea had receded from the land. So I believed that the olive branch of the Bible story was like the one with which I had appeased my nine days' hunger.

You can spend a year at sea waiting, but one day it becomes impossible to endure even another hour. The previous day I had thought I would wake up ashore. But twenty-four hours had passed and I was still looking only at the sea and the sky. Now I waited for nothing. It was my ninth night at sea. Nine days of being dead, I thought in terror—certain that at that very moment my house in Olaya in Bogotá would be filled with friends of my family. It would be the last night of the vigil. Tomorrow they would dismantle the altar and little by little they would resign themselves to the fact of my death.

Until that night I hadn't lost the faint hope that someone would remember me and try to rescue me. But when I realized that for my family it would be the ninth night of my death and the last night of my wake, I felt completely abandoned at sea. And I thought the best thing that could happen to me would be to die. I lay down in the bottom of the raft. I wanted to shout, "I'll never get up again," but the words caught in my throat. I remembered school. I raised the Virgin of Carmen medal to my lips and silently began to pray, as I thought my family would be doing just then. Then I felt all right, because I knew I was dying.

II

On the Tenth Day,
Another Hallucination: Land

My ninth night was the longest of all. I had lain down in
the raft and the waves were gently breaking against the
side. But I wasn't in command of my senses, and with every
wave that broke I relived the catastrophe. It is said that the
dying retrace their steps. Something like that happened to
me that night: In a feverish recapitulation of that dreadful day, I was on the destroyer again, lying among the
refrigerators and the stoves on the stern deck, together
with Ramón Herrera, looking at Luis Rengifo standing
watch. Each time a wave broke against the side, I felt that
the cargo was beginning to slide, that I was heading down
to the bottom of the sea, and that I was trying to swim up
toward the surface.

Then, minute by minute, my nine days of solitude,
anxiety, hunger, and thirst were replayed in sharp detail,
as if on a movie screen. First the fall, then my shipmates
shouting around the raft, then the hunger, the thirst, the

sharks, and the memories of Mobile all passed by in a succession of images. I was taking precautions against falling overboard. I saw myself again on the stern of the destroyer, trying to tie myself up so that the wave wouldn't sweep me away. I tied myself up so tightly that my wrists, my ankles, and, most of all, my right knee hurt. But though the ropes were fastened securely, the wave still came and plunged me to the bottom. When I recovered, I was swimming upward, asphyxiating.

Days before, I had thought of tying myself to the raft. That night I would have done it, but I didn't have the strength to look for the ropes of the mesh flooring. I couldn't think. For the first time in nine days I didn't know where I was. In the state I was in, it's a miracle the waves didn't drag me to the bottom that night. I wouldn't have known what was happening. I couldn't distinguish between hallucination and reality. If a wave had overturned the raft, I might have thought it was another hallucination, that I was falling off the destroyer again—as I felt many times that night—and in an instant I might have dropped into the sea and become food for the sharks that had waited patiently by the side of the raft for nine days.

But my good luck protected me again that night. I had lost my senses, reliving my nine days of solitude minute by minute, but I know now that I was as safe as if I had been lashed to the raft.

At daybreak the wind turned icy again. I had a fever. I was shivering, chilled to the bone. My right knee began to hurt. The salt from the sea had kept the wound dry but it was still raw, as on the first day, though I had taken care not to injure it further. As I lay face down, holding my knee against the floor of the raft, the wound throbbed painfully. I now believe that the wound saved my life. As if through clouds, I began to feel the pain. It forced me to take notice of my body. I felt the icy wind against my burning face. For several hours I talked a lot of nonsense, speaking to my shipmates and eating ice cream with Mary Address in a place where raucous music was playing.

After countless hours I thought that my head was about to explode. My temples throbbed and my bones ached. I could feel the rawness of the wound in my knee, which was paralyzed by swelling. It was as if my knee were immense, even larger than my body itself.

I realized I was on the raft as dawn began to break, but I didn't know how long I had been there. With great effort, I remembered I had scratched nine lines on the gunwale of the raft, but I couldn't recall when I had put the last one there. It seemed to me that a lot of time had passed since the afternoon I had eaten a root I found tangled in the webbing. Had that been a dream? There was a thick, sweet taste in my mouth, but when I tried to recall what I had eaten I couldn't remember. It hadn't given me any strength. I had eaten it all, yet my stomach was empty. I was totally spent.

How many days had passed since then? I knew day was about to dawn, but I couldn't say how many nights I had lain exhausted at the bottom of the raft, waiting for a death that seemed even more remote than land. The sky turned red, as it had the night before. That added to my confusion: I didn't know if it was dawn or twilight.

Land!

Miserable from the pain in my knee, I tried to change position. I wanted to turn around, but I couldn't do it. I was so weary that I didn't think I could stand up. So I moved my injured leg, lifted my body by bracing my hands on the bottom of the raft, and let myself fall on my back with my head resting on the side. It seemed to be dawn. I looked at my watch. It was four in the morning. Each day at that hour I would search the horizon. But I had lost all hope of sighting land. I went on scanning the sky, watching it change from bright red to pale blue. The air was still icy; I felt feverish, and my knee throbbed in excruciating pain. I lamented the fact that I hadn't died. I had no strength at all, yet I was completely alive. That made me feel lost, for I had thought I wouldn't survive the night. But I had made it and I was there as before, suffering on the raft and beginning a new day—still another day, an empty day with its intolerable sun and a pack of sharks around the raft from five o'clock on.

When the sky began to turn blue I looked at the horizon. The water was calm and green on every side. But ahead of the raft, in the half-light of dawn, I could make out a long, heavy shadow: against the bright sky I could see the outlines of coconut palms.

I was in a rage. The day before, I had been at a party in Mobile. Then I had seen a giant yellow turtle, and during the night I had been at home in Bogotá, at the La Salle de Villavicencio Academy, and with my shipmates from the destroyer. Now I was seeing land. If I had had such a hallucination four or five days earlier, I would have been wild with joy. I would have sent the raft straight to hell and leaped into the water to reach shore faster.

But now I was prepared for hallucinations. The palm trees were too distinct to be real. Moreover, they weren't at a fixed distance. Sometimes they seemed to be beside the raft; other times it looked as if they were two or three kilometers away. That was why I felt no joy. And that was what made me want to die, before I went mad from hallucinations. I looked toward the sky again. Now it was high and cloudless and an intense blue.

At a quarter to five the sun rose on the horizon. Earlier I had been frightened by the night, but now it was the new day's sun that seemed like my enemy: a gigantic and implacable enemy that came to tear up my blistered skin and drive me crazy with hunger and thirst. I cursed the sun. I cursed the day. I cursed my luck at having survived nine days adrift instead of being allowed to die of hunger or be devoured by the sharks.

Since I was in such extreme discomfort, I looked for the fragment of oar in the bottom of the raft in order to lie down on it. I had never been able to sleep on a hard pillow, but now I was searching frantically for a piece of wood half demolished by a shark.

The oar was still entwined in the rope mesh. I untied it and delicately placed it under my painful back and rested my head on the side of the raft. That was when I saw, very clearly against a rising red sun, the long green shoreline.

It was almost five. The morning was crystal clear. There couldn't be any doubt that the land was real. All the frustrated joys of the previous days—the planes, the lights of the ships, the sea gulls, the changing color of the sea— instantly came alive again at the sight of land.

If at that moment I had just finished eating two fried eggs, meat, coffee, and bread—a full breakfast aboard the destroyer—I probably would not have felt as strong as I did when I saw land. I leaped up. Ahead I clearly saw the shadow of the shoreline and the outlines of coconut palms. I didn't spot any lights. But to my right, about ten kilometers away, the first rays of the sun shone with a metallic brightness against the cliffs. Mad with joy, I grabbed my fragment of oar and tried to row toward shore in a straight line.

I calculated that the distance between the raft and shore was about two kilometers. My hands were raw, and getting up made my back hurt. But I hadn't held out for nine days—ten, counting the one just beginning—only to give up now that I saw land ahead of me. I began to sweat. The cold wind of daybreak dried my sweat and chilled me to the bone, but I kept on rowing.

But where is the shore?

The oar was useless for a raft that big. It was only a stick. It wasn't even useful as a probe to find out how deep the water was. In the first few minutes, with the abnormal strength that emotion gave me, I managed to advance a little. But then I was exhausted. I raised the oar a moment to look at the lush greenery before my eyes and I noticed that a current running parallel to the shoreline was carrying the raft along toward the cliffs.

How I regretted losing my oars! Even one of them, whole and not splintered by a shark like the piece I held in my hand, would have helped me take advantage of the current. For a few moments I thought I would have the patience to wait until the raft reached the cliffs. They glittered beneath the first sun of morning like a mountain of needles.

Luckily, I was so desperate to feel the earth under my feet that my chances of reaching them seemed too remote to bear: I later learned that those cliffs were in fact the shoals of Punta Caribana, and if the current had swept me into them, I would have been dashed against the rocks.

I tried to calculate how much strength I had left. I had to swim two kilometers to reach shore. Normally I could swim two kilometers in less than an hour. However, I didn't know how long I could swim after ten days without eating anything but a bite of fish and a root, with my body covered by blisters and with an injured knee. But it was my last chance; I didn't have time to think about it. I didn't even have time to remember the sharks. I let go of the oar, closed my eyes, and plunged into the water.

Once I hit the icy water I felt better. From that vantage I lost sight of shore. But after being in the water awhile, I realized I had made two mistakes: I hadn't taken off my shirt and I hadn't tightened my shoes. Those were the first things I had to do before starting to swim. I tried to float. I took off my shirt and tied it firmly around my waist. Then I tightened my shoelaces. Now I began to swim, desperately at first, then more calmly, realizing that with each stroke I was depleting my strength and that I still couldn't even see the shore.

I hadn't gone five meters when I realized that my chain with the Virgin of Carmen medal had come off. I stopped, and managed to grab it as I began to sink into the turbulent green water. Since I had no time to put it in my pocket, I clenched it tightly between my teeth and kept on swimming.

I felt my strength ebbing but I still couldn't see land. Then I was terrified again: maybe—no, surely—the land had been just another hallucination. The cool water had made me feel better and I was now in possession of my faculties, swimming feverishly toward an imaginary beach. But now I had covered too much distance: it was impossible to go back and look for the raft.

12

Resurrection in a Strange Land

Only after swimming furiously for fifteen minutes did I sight land again. It was still more than a kilometer away. But now I hadn't the slightest doubt that it was real and not just an apparition. The sun shone gold on the tops of the coconut palms. There were no lights on shore. There wasn't a town or a house visible from the sea. But it was land.

After twenty minutes I was exhausted, but I was sure I would make it. I swam on faith, trying not to let emotion make me lose control. I had spent half my life in the water but it wasn't until that morning of March 9 that I understood and appreciated the importance of being a good swimmer. Even though I was losing strength all the time, I kept on swimming toward shore. As I got closer, I could see the coconut palms more and more clearly.

The sun rose just as I felt I could touch bottom. I tried, but it was still too deep. Apparently I wasn't close to a beach. The water was deep very near the shore, so I had to go on swimming. I don't know exactly how long I swam. As I got closer to shore the sun heated up overhead, but it was now warming my muscles rather than punishing my skin. For the first few meters the icy water had me worrying about cramps. But my body warmed up quickly, and then the water seemed less cold and I swam with fatigue, as if in a haze, but with a spirit and a faith that prevailed over hunger and thirst.

I saw the thick foliage clearly in the weak morning sun as I tried to touch bottom a second time. The ground was right there beneath my feet. What a strange sensation it was to touch the ground after drifting at sea for ten days.

But I realized very quickly that the worst was yet to come. I was totally exhausted. I couldn't stand up. The undertow threw me back into the water, away from the beach. I had the Virgin of Carmen medal clenched between my teeth. My wet clothes and my rubber-soled shoes were terribly heavy. But even in such extreme circumstances one is modest; I thought that at any moment I might meet someone. So I went on struggling against the undertow without taking off my clothes, which hindered my progress. I was beginning to feel faint from exhaustion.

The water was above my waist. With tremendous effort, I managed to push ahead to where it was only up to my thighs. Then I decided to crawl. I dug into the sand with my hands and knees and pushed myself forward. But it was useless; the waves pushed me back. The tiny sharp grains of sand abraded the wound on my knee. I knew it was bleeding but I didn't feel pain. My fingertips were scraped raw. Even though I could feel the sand penetrate the flesh under my fingernails, I dug my fingers into it and tried to crawl forward. Very soon I felt another wave of terror: the land and the golden coconut palms began to sway before my eyes. I thought I was being swallowed up by the earth.

But that was probably an illusion brought on by exhaustion. The thought that I might be in quicksand gave me tremendous energy—a vitality born of terror—and painfully, without mercy for my raw fingertips, I went on crawling against the force of the undertow. Ten minutes later, all the suffering and hunger and thirst of ten days took their toll on my body. I lay exhausted on the warm, hard beach, not thinking about anything, not thanking anyone, not even rejoicing that, by force of will, hope, and an indefatigable desire to live, I had found this stretch of silent, unknown beach.

Human footprints

The first thing you notice on land is the silence. Before you know it, you're enveloped in a great silence. A moment later you hear the waves, distant and sad, crashing on the beach. And the murmur of the breeze amid the coconut palms heightens the feeling that you're on land. Then there is the knowledge that you've saved yourself, even if you don't know what part of the world you're in.

Once I had pulled myself together a bit, I began to look around as I lay there on the beach. The landscape was harsh. Instinctively, I looked for human footprints. There was a barbed-wire fence about twenty meters away. There was a narrow, twisting road with animal tracks on it. And next to the road there were some coconut shells.

At that moment, the slightest trace of a human presence took on the importance of revelation. Boundlessly happy, I rested my cheek on the warm sand and began to wait.

I lay there for about ten minutes. Little by little I was regaining my strength. It was after six in the morning and the sun shone brightly. Among the coconut shells along the side of the road were some whole coconuts. I crawled toward them, propped myself up on a tree trunk, and pressed one of the smooth, impenetrable fruits between my knees. Anxiously I inspected it for soft spots, as I had done with the fish five days before. With each turn I could feel the milk splash inside. The deep, guttural sound reawakened my thirst. My stomach ached, the wound on my knee was bleeding, and my fingers, raw at the tips, throbbed with a slow, deep pain. During the ten days at sea there had never been a moment when I felt I would go crazy, but I thought I would that morning as I turned the coconut round and round, trying to find a place to open it and listening to the clean, fresh, inaccessible milk splash around inside.

A coconut has three eyes at the top, arranged in a triangle. But first you have to shell the coconut with a machete to get to them. I had only my keys. Several times I tried using them to cut into the hard, tough shell, but I had no luck. Eventually I gave up. I flung the coconut away in a rage, still hearing the milk splash inside.

The road was my last hope. There at my feet the cracked shells suggested that someone came around to knock down coconuts—that someone came by every day, climbed the trees, and shelled the coconuts. And there must be an inhabited place nearby, because nobody travels a long distance just to collect a load of coconuts.

I was thinking about all that, propped up against the

tree trunk, when I heard the distant barking of a dog. My senses grew alert. I was on guard. A moment later, I thought I distinctly heard the clanging of something metallic coming closer on the road.

It was a black girl, incredibly thin, young, and dressed in white. She was carrying a little aluminum jug, the top of which was loose and jangled with every step she took. What country am I in? I wondered as I watched the black girl, who looked Jamaican, walking toward me along the road. I thought of the islands of San Andrés and Providencia. I recalled all the islands in the Antilles. This girl was my first chance, but also possibly my last. Will she understand Spanish? I wondered, trying to read the face of the girl, who, not having seen me, was distractedly scuffling along the road in her dusty leather slippers. I was so desperate not to miss my chance that the absurd thought occurred to me that she wouldn't understand me if I spoke to her in Spanish—that she would leave me there at the side of the road.

"Hello! Hello!" I said anxiously, in English.

She turned and looked at me with huge, white, fearful eyes.

"Help me!" I exclaimed, convinced she understood me.

She hesitated a moment, stared at me again, and took off like a shot, scared to death.

A man, a donkey, and a dog

I thought I would die of anxiety. In a flash I saw myself right at that spot, dead, picked apart by vultures. But then I heard the dog bark again. My heart started to pound as the barking got closer. I raised myself up on the palms of

my hands. I lifted my head. I waited. One minute. Two.
The barking grew closer. Soon there was only silence.
Then the crash of waves and the rustle of the wind in the
coconut palms. Then, after the longest minute of my life,
an emaciated dog appeared, followed by a donkey laden
with a basket on either side. Behind them walked a pale white
man wearing a straw hat and pants rolled up to his knees.
He had a rifle slung across his back.

He saw me as soon as he rounded the bend in the road,
and looked at me in surprise. He stopped. The dog, with its
tail pointing straight up, came over to sniff at me. The
man stood still, in silence. Then he unslung his rifle, planted
its butt in the ground, and went on watching me.

I don't know why, but I thought I was somewhere in
the Caribbean other than Colombia. Not certain he would
understand me, I nevertheless decided to speak Spanish to
him.

"Señor, help me," I said.

He didn't answer right away. He continued to look at
me enigmatically, without even blinking, his rifle stuck in
the ground. All I needed now was for him to shoot me, I
thought dispassionately. The dog licked my face, but I
didn't have the strength to move away.

"Help me," I repeated desperately, worried that the man
hadn't understood me.

"What happened to you?" he asked in a friendly tone
of voice.

When I heard him speak I realized that, more than
thirst, hunger, and despair, what tormented me most was
the need to tell someone what had happened to me.

Almost choking on the words, I said, without taking a
breath, "I am Luis Alejandro Velasco, one of the sailors

who fell overboard from the destroyer *Caldas* of the National Fleet on the twenty-eighth of February."

I thought the whole world would know the story. I
thought that as soon as I told him my name, the man would
be obliged to help me. But he didn't budge. He stayed
where he was, watching me, not troubling himself about
the dog, who was now licking my injured knee.

"Are you a chicken sailor?" he asked, perhaps thinking
of the merchant ships that traffic in hogs and poultry along
the coast.

"No, I'm a sailor in the Navy."

Only then did the man move. He slung the rifle across
his back again, pushed his hat back on his head, and said,
"I'm going to take some wire to the port and then I'll come
back for you." I thought this was a pretext for him to get
away.

"Are you sure you'll come back?" I asked in a pleading
voice.

The man replied that he would. He would be back.
For certain. He gave me a kindly smile and resumed walking behind the donkey. The dog stayed by my side, sniffing
me. Only when the man was a little farther away did it
occur to me to ask him, almost shouting, "What country
is this?"

And very matter-of-factly he gave the only answer I
wasn't expecting at that moment: "Colombia."

13

Six Hundred Men Take Me to San Juan

He came back, as he had promised. Even before I began waiting for him—only a little while after he left—he returned with the basket-laden donkey and the black girl with the aluminum can (his girlfriend, I learned afterward). The dog hadn't left my side. He had stopped licking my face and my wounds and had left off sniffing me. He lay at my side half asleep, not moving until he saw the donkey approach. Then he jumped up and started wagging his tail.

"Can you walk?" the man asked me.

"I'll see," I said. I tried to stand up but lost my balance.

"You can't," the man said, catching me before I fell down.

He and the girl managed to lift me onto the donkey. Supporting me under each arm, they got the animal moving. The dog ran ahead, jumping around.

There were coconuts all along the road. At sea I had been

able to endure the thirst, but here on the donkey, moving along a narrow, winding road lined with coconut palms, I felt I couldn't hold out a moment longer. I asked for some coconut milk.

"I don't have a machete," the man said.

But that wasn't so. He was carrying a machete on his belt. If I had had the strength just then, I would have taken the machete away from him by force, shelled a coconut, and eaten it whole.

Later, I found out why the man wouldn't give me any coconut milk. He had gone to a house located about two kilometers from where he had found me, and the people there advised him not to give me anything to eat until a doctor could examine me. And the nearest doctor was two days' journey from there, in San Juan de Urabá.

In less than half an hour we reached the house, a primitive structure at the side of the road, made of wood with a tin roof. Three men and two women were there. Together they helped me off the donkey, took me to a bedroom, and put me in a canvas hammock. One of the women went to the kitchen, brought back a little pot of cinnamon-flavored boiled water, and sat down at the edge of the bed to feed me spoonfuls of it. I drank the first few drops greedily. With the next few I felt I was regaining my spirit. Then I didn't want any more to drink; I wanted only to tell them what had happened to me.

No one knew about the accident. I tried to explain, to give the whole story so they'd know how I'd been saved. I'd had the idea that in whatever part of the world I turned up, everyone would already know about the catastrophe. It was disillusioning to realize, as the woman spoon-fed me cinnamon water like a sick child, that I had been mistaken.

Several times I insisted on telling them what had happened. Impassive, the men and women sat at the foot of the bed, watching me. It seemed like a ceremony. If I hadn't been so happy to be saved from the sharks and all the other dangers of the sea I had endured for ten days, I would have thought that they were from another planet.

Believing the story

The kind manner of the woman who fed me wouldn't permit any distractions from her purpose. Each time I tried to tell my story she said, "Be quiet now. You can tell us later."

I would have eaten anything. From the kitchen came the aroma of lunch being prepared. But all my pleading was useless.

"After the doctor sees you, we'll give you something to eat," they said.

But the doctor did not arrive. Every ten minutes they gave me little spoonfuls of sugar water. The younger of the women, a girl, cleaned my wounds with cloths and warm water. The day passed slowly. And gradually I began to feel better. I was sure I was in the care of friendly people. If they had given me food instead of doling out spoonfuls of sugar water, my body wouldn't have withstood the shock.

The man I had met on the road was named Dámaso Imitela. At ten o'clock on the morning of March 9, the day I landed on the beach, he went to the station house in nearby Mulatos and returned with several policemen to the house where he had brought me. They knew nothing about the tragedy either. No one had heard the news in Mulatos; newspapers don't reach them there. In a little store where they've installed an electric motor, they've got a refrigerator and a radio. But they don't listen to the news. As I learned later, when Dámaso Imitela reported to the police inspector that he had found me lying exhausted on the beach and that I had said I was from the destroyer *Caldas*, they turned on the motor and listened to news programs from Cartagena all day. But by then there was nothing about the accident. There had been only a brief mention the evening it occurred.

The police inspector, all the policemen, and sixty men from Mulatos got together to help me. A little after midnight they came to the house, and their conversation woke me from virtually the only sound sleep I had had in the last twelve days.

Before dawn the house was filled with people. All of Mulatos, men, women, and children, came to get a look at me. That was my first contact with a crowd of curiosity seekers, the kind who in subsequent days would follow me everywhere. The crowd carried lanterns and flashlights. When the police inspector, together with almost all his companions, moved me from the bed, it felt as if they were tearing away my sunburned skin. It was a real scramble.

It was hot. I felt I was suffocating in the crowd of protective faces. When I walked out to the road, a sea of lanterns and flashlights spotlighted my face. I was blinded in the midst of the murmuring throng and the loud orders of the police inspector. I couldn't imagine when I might reach some destination. Since the day I fell off the destroyer, I had done nothing but travel an unknown route. That morning I went on traveling, not knowing where, unable even to imagine what that diligent, friendly crowd was going to do with me.

The tale of the fakir

The road to Mulatos from the place where they had found me is long and arduous. They put me in a hammock supported by two poles. Two men at the ends of each pole carried me along a narrow, twisting road lit by lanterns. We were in the open air, but it was as hot as a closed room, because of the lanterns.

Relays of eight men traded places every half hour. Then they'd give me a little water and bits of soda biscuit. I wanted to know where we were going and what they were going to do with me. They talked about everything but that. Everyone spoke except me. The inspector, who led the crowd, wouldn't let anyone get close enough to talk to me. I could hear shouts, orders, and conversation in the distance. When we reached the main street of Mulatos, the police couldn't handle the crowd. It was about eight o'clock in the morning.

Mulatos is a fishing hamlet and has no telegraph office. The nearest town is San Juan de Urabá, where a small plane from Montería lands twice a week. When we reached the hamlet I felt I had arrived somewhere. I thought I would receive news of my family. But Mulatos was barely the midpoint of my journey.

I was put in a house and the whole town lined up to get a look at me. I thought of a fakir I had seen for fifty centavos in Bogotá about two years earlier. You had to stand in line for several hours to get a look at him. You moved about two feet every half hour. When you reached the room where the fakir was displayed in a glass box, you no longer wanted to look at anybody, you just wanted to get out immediately, stretch your legs, and breathe fresh air.

The only difference between the fakir and me was that the fakir was in a glass box. He hadn't eaten for nine days. I had been ten days at sea and one day in bed in a room in Mulatos. I watched the faces parade before me —black faces, white faces—in an endless line. The heat was terrible. Then the appropriate response came to me—a sense of humor about it all—and I guessed that someone might even be selling tickets to see the shipwrecked sailor.

They took me to San Juan de Urabá in the same hammock in which they had carried me to Mulatos. But the crowd accompanying me had grown: there were no fewer than six hundred men. There were also women, children, and animals. Some were on donkeys but most were on foot. The trip took almost all day. Carried by that crowd, by six hundred men taking turns along the way, I felt my strength returning. I think Mulatos was left depopulated. From the early hours of morning, the motor had been turned on, and the radio had filled the hamlet with music. It was like a festival. At the center of it all, and the reason for the festival, I had lain in bed while the whole town streamed by to look at me. That same crowd couldn't bear to send me off alone, but had to go with me to San Juan de Urabá in a long caravan as wide as the winding road. I was hungry and thirsty during the whole trip. The little bits of soda biscuit and the minute sips of water brought me around again but had also stimulated my hunger and thirst. Entering San Juan reminded me of a village feast. All the inhabitants of that picturesque little town buffeted by the sea winds came out to meet me. The town had taken precautions against the curiosity seekers. The police managed to contain the mob that elbowed one another in the streets trying to get a look at me.

This was the end of my journey. Dr. Humberto Gómez, the first physician to give me a thorough examination, passed on the great news; he didn't tell me anything before finishing his examination because he wanted to make sure I could handle it. Cuffing me lightly on the cheek and smiling amiably, he said, "There's a plane ready to take you to Cartagena. Your family is waiting for you there."

14

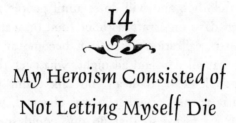

My Heroism Consisted of
Not Letting Myself Die

It never occurred to me that a man could become a hero
for being on a raft ten days and enduring hunger and
thirst. I had no choice. If the raft had been outfitted with
water, vacuum-packed biscuits, a compass, and fishing
gear, I surely would have been as alive as I am now. But
there would be a difference: I wouldn't have been treated
like a hero. So, in my case, heroism consisted solely of not
allowing myself to die of hunger and thirst for ten days.

I did nothing heroic. All my effort went toward saving
myself. But since salvation came wrapped in a glow and
with the title of hero as a prize, like a bonbon with a surprise inside it, I had no choice but to accept my salvation
as it came, heroism and all.

I have been asked how it feels to be a hero. I never know
how to respond. So far as I'm concerned, I feel the same as
I did before. Nothing has changed internally or externally.
The terrible burns from the sun have stopped hurting. The

knee injury has become scar tissue. I am Luis Alejandro Velasco again, and that's enough for me.

It's other people who have changed. My friends are now friendlier than before. And I imagine that my enemies are worse enemies, although I don't really think I have any. When people recognize me on the street, they stare at me as if I were some strange animal. For that reason I dress in civilian clothes, and will do so until people forget that I spent ten days on a raft without food or water.

Your first realization when you become an important person is that all day and all night, whatever the circumstances, people want to hear you talk about yourself. I learned that at the Cartagena Naval Hospital, where they assigned me a guard so that no one could speak to me. After three days I felt completely normal again but I couldn't leave the hospital. I knew that after I was discharged I would have to tell my story to the whole world, because, as the guards had told me, newspaper reporters from all over the country had come to the city to interview and photograph me. One of them, with an impressive mustache about twenty centimeters long, took more than fifty photos, but he wasn't permitted to ask me anything about my adventure.

Another one, more daring, disguised himself as a doctor, fooled the guards, and slipped into my room. It was a great coup for him, but short-lived.

The story of a news story

Only my father, the guards, and the doctors and nurses at the naval hospital were permitted in my room. One day, a doctor I had never seen before came in. He looked very young in his smock and eyeglasses, with a phonendoscope hanging from his neck. He turned up unannounced, saying nothing.

The corporal of the guard looked at him in perplexity and asked him to identify himself. The young doctor searched his pockets, stalled a little, and said he had forgotten his papers. Then the guard told him he couldn't talk to me without special permission from the director of the hospital. So they went off in search of the director. Twenty minutes later, they came back to my room.

The guard entered first and told me that the man had been given permission to examine me for fifteen minutes and that he was a psychiatrist from Bogotá. The guard, however, thought he was a reporter in disguise.

"Why do you think so?" I asked him.

"Because he's very frightened. And psychiatrists don't use a phonendoscope."

Nonetheless, he had talked to the director of the hospital for fifteen minutes. They would have spoken about medicine and psychiatry in complicated medical terms and quickly reached an understanding.

I don't know if it was because of the guard's warning, but when the young doctor came back to my room I no longer thought of him as a medical man. He didn't seem like a reporter either, although I had never seen a reporter until that moment. He looked to me like a priest disguised as a doctor. It struck me that he didn't know how to begin, but in fact he was trying to figure out how to distract the guard.

"Do me a favor and find me a piece of paper," he said to the guard.

He probably thought the guard would go to the office to look for paper. But the guard's orders were not to leave me alone. Rather than go looking for it, he went to the corridor and called out: "Bring some writing paper on the double."

A moment later, the paper arrived. More than five minutes had gone by and the doctor still hadn't asked me a question. The examination didn't begin until the paper arrived. He handed me the paper and asked me to draw a ship. I drew a ship. Then he asked me to sign the drawing, which I did. Next he asked me to draw a farmhouse. I drew a house as best I could, with a banana plant next to it. He asked me to sign the drawing. That was when I became convinced he was a reporter in disguise. But he insisted he was a doctor.

When I finished drawing he examined the papers, mumbled a few words, and began to ask questions about my adventure. But the guard intervened to remind him that that kind of question was not permitted. Then he examined my body, the way a doctor does. His hands were ice cold. If the guard had touched them, he would have thrown the man out of the room. But I said nothing, because his nervousness and the possibility that he might be a reporter aroused my sympathy. Before his fifteen minutes were up he hurried out, taking the drawings with him.

All hell broke loose the next day. The drawings appeared on the front page of *El Tiempo*, complete with captions and arrows. "This is where I went overboard," read one caption, with an arrow pointing toward the ship's bridge. Which was an error, because I had been on the stern, not on the bridge. But the drawings were mine.

I was told that I should ask for a correction. That I could demand one. But that seemed absurd. I felt great admiration for a reporter who would disguise himself as a doctor to gain entrance to a military hospital. If he had found a way to let me know he was a reporter, I would have known how to get rid of the guard. Because, in fact, I had already been given permission that day to tell my story.

The business of the story

The adventure of the reporter in disguise gave me a very good idea of how much interest the newspapers had in the story of my ten days at sea. Everyone was interested. My own friends asked me to tell it many times. When I got to Bogotá, now almost fully recovered, I realized that my life had changed. I was greeted with great fanfare at the airport. I was decorated by the president of the country—he congratulated me on my heroic feat. From that day on, I knew I would remain in the Navy, but now with the rank of cadet.

In addition, there was something I hadn't anticipated: offers from advertising and publicity agencies. I was very grateful for my watch, which had kept perfect time during my odyssey, but I didn't think that would be of much interest to the watch manufacturer. Nonetheless, they gave me five hundred pesos and a new watch. For using a certain brand of chewing gum and saying so in an ad, I received a thousand pesos. I was lucky that the manufacturer of my shoes gave me two thousand pesos for endorsing them in an ad. For permitting my story to be told on radio I received five thousand. I never imagined that surviving ten days of hunger and thirst would turn out to be so profitable. But it is: up till now I have received almost ten thousand pesos. Nevertheless, I wouldn't relive that adventure for a million.

My hero's life is nothing extraordinary. I get up at ten o'clock in the morning. I go to a café to chat with my friends, or to one of the agencies working on ads about my adventure. I go to the movies almost every day. And I'm never alone. But I can't reveal the name of my companion, for that belongs to the rest of my story.

Every day I receive letters from all over. Letters from people I don't know. From Pereira, bearing the initials J.V.C., I received a long poem about rafts and sea gulls. Mary Address, who had a mass said for the repose of my soul when I was adrift in the Caribbean, writes to me frequently. She sent me an inscribed photograph, which newspaper readers have seen.

I have told my story on television and on a radio program. I've also told it to my friends. I told it to an elderly widow with a huge photograph album who invited me to her home. Some people tell me this story is a fantasy. And I ask them: If it is, then what did I do during my ten days at sea?

A NOTE ON THE TYPE

This book was set on the Linotype in Janson, a recutting made direct from type cast from matrices long thought to have been made by the Dutchman Anton Janson, who was a practicing type founder in Leipzig during the years 1668–87. However, it has been conclusively demonstrated that these types are actually the work of Nicholas Kis (1650–1702), a Hungarian, who most probably learned his trade from the master Dutch type founder Dirk Voskens. The type is an excellent example of the influential and sturdy Dutch types that prevailed in England up to the time William Caslon (1692–1766) developed his own incomparable designs from them.

Composed by Maryland Linotype, Inc.,
Baltimore, Maryland

Typography and binding design by
Tasha Hall